Heritage Crochet for Your Home

Heritage Crochet
for Your Home

Kathy Grin

Kangaroo Press

To my grandchildren, who will one day, I hope, enjoy the craft of crochet
as much as I do.

Acknowledgments

This book would not have been possible without the help of many, and I want to thank all those for whose assistance I am most grateful.
• Furze Hewitt, who first sowed the seed of this book in my mind and then, when the book started to eventuate, gave me so much practical advice.
• Bob Rodda for his superb photography. For him, as for me, this book is a first.
• Eleonor Cole for her delightful drawings. She seemed to know just what I wanted, which I found so difficult to put into words. For Eleonor this book is a first also.

• Elaine Lawson, curator of Lanyon Homestead, and her staff, for the use of Lanyon Homestead for the photography and all the assistance given during the photographic session.
• Sue George and Val Taylor for lending me crochet books which had belonged to their mothers and grandmothers.
• Milica Byrne of ABC - Bits and Bytes Processing for her work with this book.
   Last, but not least, I want to thank my sons and my daughter-in-law, Mary, for the encouragement and assistance given to me when writing this book.

The photographs in this book were taken at Lanyon Homestead in the Australian Capital Territory, south of Canberra. Andrew Cunningham's 1895 homestead has been furnished to recreate the country lifestyle of mid-nineteenth century Australia

© Kathy Grin 1995
First published in 1995 by Kangaroo Press Pty Ltd
3 Whitehall Road Kenthurst NSW 2156 Australia
PO Box 6125 Dural Delivery Centre NSW 2158
Printed in Hong Kong through Colorcraft Ltd

ISBN 0 86417 674 0

Contents

INTRODUCTION

My aim in writing this book was firstly to preserve the beautiful crochet patterns of our forebears and secondly to translate them in today's English. Little did I realise the mammoth task I was undertaking.

Researching this book was a fascinating experience. There are so many beautiful patterns and so many very intricate patterns - this book touches only the tip of the iceberg. For years I'd been collecting old crochet patterns from the nineteenth and early twentieth centuries. I noted how often only white was used, and I asked myself: Why is that? Maybe it was because years ago nuns were the ones who crocheted, and white was the sign of holiness and purity. Or maybe it was because cotton is naturally white and dying was expensive. We don't know and it does not really matter. Laying a white crochet doily on a dark wooden table reveals the delicacy of the patterns in the work, a point emphasised very strongly when we used the beautiful old furniture at Lanyon Homestead as a background for the photography.

All the items in this book have been made in white cotton because I love its clear crispness, and it always looks so fresh. That does not mean that you can't use colours for crochet. Go ahead if you love colour. It is very much a matter of personal preference.

The history of crochet is very vague because little has been written about it. How old is it? Who invented it? Little early crochet has survived, because for a long time crochet was regarded as a working-class craft, not worth preserving.

The earliest concrete information about crochet dates from the 1840s, and it took the Irish Potato Famine to bring this about. The two-year period when the potato, the staple diet of the Irish, rotted in the fields was, particularly for the working class Irish, catastrophic. The women tried very hard to earn some extra money when their regular farm livelihood collapsed. The nuns taught many women to crochet in imitation of the European laces so much sought after by the gentry. Even today Irish crochet is beautiful and very special. The closest I have come in this book to Irish crochet is the milk jug cover 'Janny' on page 70 with the Irish rose in the centre.

Not for another twenty years did crochet become popular with upper class women. Queen Victoria learned to crochet and was seen to crochet in public. Crochet has been in and out of fashion ever since. For a time it was regarded as old-fashioned in English-speaking countries, but in Europe hand crochet has never been out of fashion. Anyone who has travelled in Europe has seen the beautiful crisp white crochet curtains in the windows, particularly in Holland.

Crochet here in Australia (and probably worldwide) is experiencing a strong resurgence of popularity. Crochet is one of the easiest handcrafts to learn. It is a simple technique which produces quick and satisfying results. Once you learn to handle the crochet hook and yarn, and master the few basic stitches, you will quickly improve both in skill and speed. Thread and crochet hook are the only materials needed.

Crochet is a locked stitch. It will not unravel and cannot be made by machine. Although yarns vary and each person has a different way of working you will all have the same result no matter what your aim is: your own beautiful hand made items.

Crochet hooks are normally made of steel or plastic —the smaller sizes in steel, the larger ones in plastic. The size required depends on the thickness and type of thread you work with. The thicker the thread, the larger the hook used. Tight workers should use a larger hook than the one specified in a pattern and loose workers a smaller hook. It is important to always check your tension by crocheting a small sample first. The size of the hook you use is not the most important thing as long as your sample has the same numbers of stitches as in the pattern.

Crocheting is quick, easy, versatile and relaxing. It can be used in so many creative and practical ways to fashion presents and home furnishings.

Kathy Grin

HANDY HINTS

Common Mistakes

1. Keep your work straight. At the beginning of a row the turning chain is counted as the first stitch. At the end, the turning chain counts as the last stitch. That means the last stitch in any row must be made in the turning chain.
2. Don't change your tension as you work. Crochet should be fairly tight, but not so tight you have difficulty getting the hook through. Loose work stretches, while tight work loses its elasticity.
3. Never knot the thread. Leave about 7.5 cm (3") of thread and darn it into the work with a tapestry needle.
4. Untidy seams and careless finishing off can spoil the best made crocheted article. Take time and care when pressing and making up.

Mounting Crochet Onto Linen
Sew a narrow hem all around linen, incorporating a spoke stitch or drawn thread finish; dc around linen, working 3dc in each corner. If your work pulls, work 1ch between each dc.
Oversew crochet neatly onto dc edge.

Beginning of Rounds and Rows
Always begin each rnd or row with 3ch for first treble, 4ch for first dbl tr or 5ch for first tr tr.
When working in rounds, always close the round with a slip stitch.

Making Up
If your work becomes soiled, wash it gently in mild soapy suds, rinse well and roll in a towel to soak up the excess water, then pin it out on a clean towel with rust-proof pins. Don't pull so hard that it distorts your work. Let it dry naturally, if necessary overnight.

I never iron crochet articles while they are dry. Dampen them, roll in a towel for at least an hour, then pin on a clean town to dry. If you prefer to iron your crochet work, iron it when damp, from the centre out. With care your doilies and cloths will look like new, even after years of use.

Look after your precious hand-crocheted work and it will give you a lifetime of pleasure.

Australian and American Terms

Beginners can become very confused trying to make sense of different terms for stitches in different patterns. Australia uses the English and European terms for stitches, which differ from those used in America. The actual method of making the stitches is exactly the same. The following table gives the English and American names for the same stitches.

Australian (English)	American
Chain	Chain
Slip stitch	Slipstitch
Double crochet	Single crochet
Half treble	Half double crochet
Treble	Double crochet
Double treble	Treble

Abbreviations

alt = alternatively	pat = pattern
beg = beginning	rep = repeat/ing
ch = chain	RH = right hand
ch-lp = chain loop	rnd/s = round/s
cl = cluster	RS = right side
cont = continue/ing	sc = single crochet
dc = double crochet	sl = slip
dec = decrease/ing	sl st = slip stitch
dbl tr = double treble	sp/s = space/s
foll = follow/ing	st/s = stitch/es
grp/s = group/s	tog = together
htr = half treble	tr = treble
inc = increase	tr tr = triple treble
incl = inclusive	WS = wrong side
LH = left hand	yoh = yarn over hook
p/s = picots	yrh = yarn round hook

* repeat instructions following the asterisk as many times as directed.
( ) work directions within brackets as many times as specified.

CROCHET STITCHES AND VARIATIONS

These directions are written for right-handed workers.
Left-handers will need to reverse the directions.

Chain stitch (ch)

The basis of every crochet pattern is the chain stitch - one loop pulled through another loop.

1. Loop thread over your third finger, under middle finger of your left hand. This keeps the tension firm. (People who have done some crocheting before may hold their thread differently. This does not matter as long as your tension is even.)
2. Hold thread between thumb and forefinger of left hand and make a loop. Hold loop in place.
3. With your right hand hold hook between thumb and forefinger (as if you were holding a pen).
4. Begin with a slip loop on the hook. Insert hook behind the vertical strand as shown, then pull the ends of the yarn to tighten the loop (but not too tight).
5. Hold hook with slip loop in your right hand and control yarn with your left hand. Bringing the hook towards you, take it under then over the top of the yarn in your left hand, so catching it in the curve of the hook. This is called 'yarn around hook' (yrh).

6. Holding knot of slip loop firmly between thumb and forefinger of your left hand, draw yarn from back to front through slip loop, completing one chain (ch). One working loop always remains on the hook.

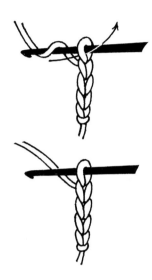

Repeat steps 4, 5 and 6 until you have the length of chain needed. Always hold the stitch you have just made and let the yarn run smoothly through your left hand. Make the chain stitches fairly loose, as a tight start will affect the finished product.

Slip stitch (sl st)

This is a shallow stitch used to relocate the yarn without making the item longer; it is also used in joining motifs together.

1. Insert the hook in the usual way into the chain or stitch.

2. Wind yarn around the hook.

3. Draw yarn through chain or stitch and the loop on the hook.

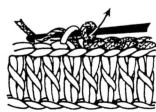

Note: In all crochet, pick up two horizontal loops of each stitch unless the pattern says otherwise.

Double crochet (dc)

After making the required number of chains plus one extra (turning chain) you start making the first row.

1. Insert the hook from front to back into the third chain from the hook.
2. Wind the yarn around the hook from the back.
3. Draw a loop through the chain making two loops on the hook.
4. Wind the yarn around the hook again and draw it through both loops on the hook.
5. Repeat this till you have reached the end of the chain.
6. Turn the work from right to left (the last stitch becomes the first).
7. Make one turning chain to count as the first dc in the row.
8. Work each stitch in the previous row by inserting the hook into the two horizontal loops at the top of the stitch.
9. Continue till you reach the end of the row.
Repeat these steps.

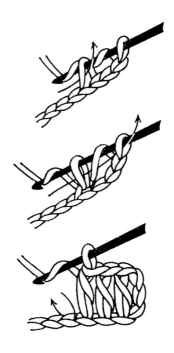

Half treble (htr)

1. Wind yarn around the hook.
2. Insert the hook into chain and draw the loop through the chain so making three loops on the hook.
3. Wind yarn around again and draw through all three loops.

To work the second row make two chains when turning the work. The two chains count as the first stitch.

Treble (tr)

1. Wind yarn around the hook.
2. Insert the hook into chain and draw loop through, making three loops on the hook.
3. Wind yarn again and draw through the first two loops, leaving two loops on the hook.
4. Wind yarn around again and draw it through the remaining two loops.

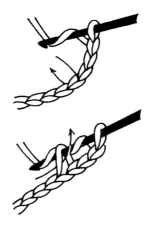

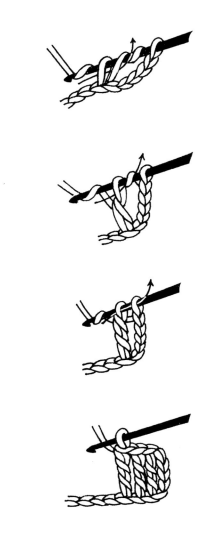

To begin the second row make three chains before turning your work. These are the first stitch of the next row.

Double treble (dbl tr)
There are four steps in this stitch.
1. Wind yarn twice around the hook.
2. Insert the hook into chain and draw a loop through (you have now four loops on your hook).
3. Wind yarn around the hook again and draw it through the first two loops. (You now have three loops on your hook).
4. Repeat step 2 so there are two loops on the hook.
5. Wind yarn around the hook again and draw it through the two remaining loops. A single loop remains on the hook.

Work four chains when turning the work. This is the first stitch of the next row.

Note: When working a triple treble (tr tr) you wind the yarn three times around the hook.

Picot (p)
This is a decorative stitch. Picots form an attractive edging or filling.
1. Work three chain stitches.
2. Make a slip stitch or double crochet in the two loops at the base of the first stitch.

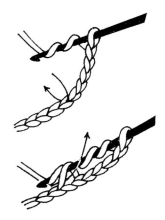

Treble cluster and puff stitches

Treble cluster and puff stitches, and the popcorn stitch, are simple variations of the treble stitch, and can be followed from the diagrams.

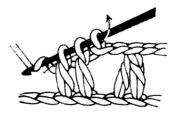

2 treble cluster

puff stitch

Popcorn stitch

1. Four trebles into one chain loop.
2. Drop loop from the hook.
3. Insert the hook into top of first treble.
4. Draw the dropped loop through.

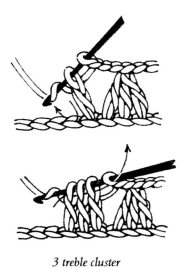

3 treble cluster

THE PATTERNS

DOILIES

Starflower

27 cm (10½") round doily

Materials: 1 x 20g ball DMC No 40
crochet hook No 0.75

Commence with 8ch, close with sl st to form a ring.
1st rnd: ★ 3dbl tr cluster, 6ch; repeat from ★ 5 times (6 3dbl tr cls made).
2nd rnd: ★ (1dbl tr, 3ch) twice, 1tr halfway in stem of last dbl tr (to form a Y), 3ch, 1dbl tr; repeat from ★ close with a sl st.
3rd rnd: ★ 4ch (for first tr), 3ch, in 3ch of Y work 3dbl tr cl 3ch (1dbl tr, 3ch) twice and 3dbl tr cl, 3ch; repeat from ★ close with sl st.
4th rnd: 1dc in same place as last sl st, ★ 3ch, (3dbl tr cl, 3ch) twice in each of next three 3ch sps, 3ch, 1dc in next tr; repeat from ★ close with sl st in dc.
5th rnd: ★ 2tr in same dc, 2ch, (2tr in 3dbl tr cl, 2ch, 2tr in next sp, 2ch) 5 times, 2tr in cl, 2ch, 2tr in dc; repeat from ★ close with sl st.
6th rnd: sl st into first space, ★ 1tr 3ch 1tr in each 2ch sp of scallop (10 repeats); repeat from ★ 5 more times, close with sl st.
7th rnd: sl st into sp, 1dc in same sp, ★ (7ch, 1dc in next sp) 9 times, 1dc in sp; repeat from ★ ending with 3ch, 1dbl tr in first dc.
8th rnd: 1dc in same sp, ★ 7ch, 1dc in next sp; repeat from ★ ending with 3ch, 1dbl tr in first dc.

9th rnd: 1dc in same place, ★ 8ch, 1dc in next sp; repeat from ★ ending with 3ch, 1dbl tr in first dc.
10th rnd: 3ch (for first tr) 2tr in same sp, ★ 3ch, 3tr in next sp; repeat from ★ ending with 3ch, close with sl st in last of 3ch.
11th rnd: ★ 3tr, 2ch, 1dc in sp, 2ch; repeat from ★ close with sl st.
12th rnd: ★ 3tr, 5ch; repeat from ★ close with sl st.
13th rnd: sl st to 2nd tr, 1dc in same tr, ★ 3 tr in centre of 5ch lp, 3ch, 1dc in 2nd tr, 3ch; repeat from ★ close with sl st in first dc.
14th rnd: as 12th rnd.
15th rnd: as 13th rnd.
16th rnd: as 12th rnd.
17th rnd: as 13th rnd.
18th rnd: as 12th rnd.
19th rnd: as 13th rnd.
20th rnd: sl st over 2tr, 3ch (for first tr), 1tr 2ch 2tr in 2nd tr of previous rnd, ★ 4ch, 2tr 2ch 2tr in second tr of next 3 trs; repeat from ★ close with sl st.
21st rnd: sl st into 2ch sp, 1dc in same sp, ★ 3ch, in next 4ch sp work 3dbl tr cl (3ch 1dbl tr) twice and 3dbl tr cl, 3ch, 1dc in 2ch sp; repeat from ★ close with sl st.
22nd rnd: 3ch (for first tr), 3ch, ★ in each 3ch sp work 3dbl tr cl 3ch 3dbl tr cl, 3ch, 1tr in 3ch sp; repeat from ★ close with sl st.
Fasten off.

Aster

18 cm (7") round doily

Materials: 1 x 20g ball DMC No 40
crochet hook No 0.75

Commence with 6ch, close with sl st to form a ring.
1st rnd: work 8dc in ring, close with sl st.
2nd rnd: 6ch, ★ 1tr in next dc, 3ch; repeat from ★ close with sl st.
3rd rnd: 4ch, 1dbl tr in same place as last sl st, ★ 7ch, 2dbl tr cl in next tr; repeat from ★ ending with 7ch, close with sl st in 1st dbl tr.

4th rnd: sl st into first lp, 4ch (for first dbl tr), 4dbl tr in same sp, ★ 5ch, 5dbl tr in next lp; repeat from ★ ending with 5ch, close with sl st.

5th rnd: sl st to 3rd dbl tr, 7ch, dbl tr in same place as sl st, ★ 5dbl tr with 1ch between each in next 5ch sp, skip 2dbl tr, 1dbl tr 3ch and 1dbl tr in next dbl tr; repeat from ★ omitting 1dbl tr 3ch and 1dbl tr at end of last repeat, close with sl st in 4th of 7ch.

6th rnd: sl st in first sp, 4ch, 2dbl tr 5ch and 3dbl tr in same sp, ★ 9ch, 3dbl tr 5ch 3dbl tr in next 3ch sp; repeat from ★ ending with 9ch, close with sl st.

7th rnd: 3ch, 1tr in each of next 2dbl tr, ★ 1tr in each of next 2ch, 3tr in next ch, 1tr in each of next 2ch, 1tr in each of 3dbl tr, 1tr in each of next 4ch, 3tr in next ch, 1tr in each of next 4ch, 1tr in each of next 3dbl tr; repeat from ★ omitting 3tr at end of last repeat, close with sl st.

8th rnd: sl st over 6tr, 7ch, 1dbl tr in same place as last sl st, ★ 5ch, skip 5tr, 1tr in next tr, 5ch, skip 5tr, 1dbl tr 3ch 1dbl tr in next tr; repeat from ★ omitting 1dbl tr 3ch 1dbl tr at end of last repeat, close with sl st in 4th of 7ch.

9th rnd: 3ch, ★ 1tr in next ch, 3tr in next ch, 1 tr in next ch, 1tr in next dbl tr, 1tr in each of next 4ch, leaving the last lp of each on hook work 1tr in next ch, skip 1tr, 1tr in next ch, yoh and draw through all lps on hook, 1tr in each of next 4ch, 1tr in dbl tr; repeat from ★ omitting 1tr at end of last repeat, close with sl st.

10th rnd: sl st over next 3tr, 5ch, 1dbl tr 1ch 1dbl tr in same place as last sl st, 5ch, (1dbl tr 1ch) twice and 2dbl tr in same place, ★1ch, skip 7tr, 1dbl tr 5ch 1dbl tr in next joint tr, 1ch, skip 7tr, in next tr work (1dbl tr 1ch) twice and 1dbl tr, 5ch, (1dbl tr 1ch) twice and 1dbl tr; repeat from ★ ending with 1ch, skip 7tr, 1dbl tr 5ch and 1dbl tr in joint tr, 1ch, close with sl st in 4th of 5ch.

11th rnd: sl st over next 4sts, sl st into next 5ch sp, 5ch (for first dbl tr), in same space work 5dbl tr with 1ch between each, ★ 1ch, 1dbl tr 5ch and 1dbl tr in next 5ch sp, 1ch, in next 5ch sp work 6dbl tr with 1ch between each; repeat from ★ ending with 1ch, 1dbl tr 5ch 1dbl tr in next 5ch sp, 1ch, close with sl st in 4th of 5ch.

12th rnd: 5ch, ★ (1dbl tr in next dbl tr, 1ch) twice, 1dbl tr 1ch and 1dbl tr in next 1ch sp, (1ch, 1dbl tr in next dbl tr) 3 times, 4ch, 1dc in next 5ch sp, 4ch, skip 1dbl tr, 1dbl tr in next dbl tr, 1ch; repeat from ★ omitting 1dbl tr and 1ch at end of last repeat, close with sl st in 4th of 5ch.

13th rnd: 5ch, ★ (1dbl tr in next dbl tr, 1ch) 3 times, 1dbl tr 3ch and 1dbl tr in next sp, (1ch, 1dbl tr in next dbl tr) 4 times, 1dbl tr in next dbl tr, 1ch; repeat from ★ omitting 1dbl tr and 1ch at end of last repeat, close with sl st in 4th of 5ch.

14th rnd: 1ch, ★ (1dc in next sp, 1dc in next dbl tr) 4 times, 3dc in next sp, 1dc in next dbl tr, 1dc in next sp) 4 times, 1 dc in each of next 2dbl tr; repeat from ★ omitting 1dc at end of last repeat, close with sl st.

15th rnd: ★ (1dc in next dc, 3ch, 1tr in same place as last dc, skip 1dc) 9 times, 1dc in next dc, skip 2dc; repeat from ★ close with sl st.
Fasten off.

Tulip

20 cm (8") round doily

Materials: 1 x 20g ball DMC No 40
crochet hook No 0.75

Note: Begin each round with 3ch for first treble.
Commence with 10ch, close with sl st to form a ring.
1st rnd: 24dc in ring.
2nd rnd: ★ 1tr, 1ch; repeat from ★ close with sl st.
3rd rnd: sl st into 1ch sp, 1dc in same sp, ★ 4ch, 1dc in next sp; repeat from ★ ending with 4ch, close with sl st.
4th rnd: sl st to centre of 4ch lp, 1dc in same lp, ★ 5ch, 1dc in next lp, repeat from ★ ending with 2ch 1tr for last lp.
5th rnd: 1dc in same lp, ★ 6ch, 1dc in next lp; repeat from ★ ending with 2ch 1dbl tr for last lp.
6th rnd: 3tr in same lp, ★ 7ch, 3tr in next lp; repeat from ★ close with 3ch 1dbl tr for last lp.
7th and 8th rnds: 1dc in same lp, ★ 8ch, 1dc in next lp, repeat from ★ ending with 3ch 1dbl tr for last lp.
9th rnd: 3tr in same lp, ★ 7ch, 3tr in next lp; repeat from ★ ending with 3ch 1tr tr for last lp.
10th rnd: 1dc in each tr, 7dc over each 7ch lp, close with sl st.
11th rnd: sl st to first dc of lp, ★ 1tr in second dc, 1ch; repeat from ★ close with sl st (120tr made).
12th rnd: sl st to next tr, ★ 1tr in tr, 2tr in sp, 1tr in tr, 8ch, skip 4sps, 8ch, skip 4sps; repeat from ★ close with sl st.
13th rnd: ★ 1tr in each of next 4tr, 7ch, in dbl tr work (1dbl tr 3 ch) twice and 1dbl tr, 7ch; repeat from ★ close with sl st.
14th rnd: sl st to second tr, ★ 2tr, 7ch 1dbl tr in dbl tr, 5ch 5dbl tr in centre dbl tr, 5ch, 1dbl tr in next dbl tr, 7ch; repeat from ★ ending with 4ch 1dbl tr for last lp.
15th rnd: ★ 7ch, 1dc in centre of next lp, 5ch, skip next dbl tr, in each of next 5dbl tr work 1tr tr and 2tr worked into the stem of each tr tr, 5ch, skip next dbl tr, 1dc in centre of 7ch lp; repeat from ★ close with 3ch 1dbl tr for last lp.
16th rnd: 1dc in same lp, ★ 7ch, (3dbl tr cl, 5ch) 4 times, 3dbl tr cl, 7ch, 1dc in 7ch lp; repeat from ★ close with sl st.
17th rnd: sl st over 5ch, ★ 2dbl tr, in each 5ch lp work (1dbl tr 1 picot, 1dbl tr) twice, 2dbl tr in next 2ch; repeat from ★ close with sl st.
Fasten off.

Potpourri

27 cm (10½") round doily

Materials: 1 x 20g ball DMC No 40
crochet hook No 0.75

Note: Begin each round with 3ch for first tr, and 5ch for tr tr.

Commence with 6ch, close with sl st to form a ring.
1st rnd: (2tr tr cl, 5ch) 8 times, close with sl st.
2nd rnd: sl st into 5ch sp, in each 5ch sp work (1tr, 1ch) 4 times and 1tr, close with sl st.
3rd rnd: sl st into 1ch sp, 1dc in same sp, ★ 2ch, 1dc in next sp, 3ch, 1dc in next sp, 2ch, 1dc in next sp, skip 2tr, 1dc in next sp; repeat from ★ close with sl st.
4th rnd: ★ 1dc in 2ch sp, 4ch, 2tr in 3ch sp, 4ch, 1dc in next sp, 4ch; repeat from ★ close with sl st.
5th rnd: sl st over 3ch, ★ 1dc in next ch, 1dc in each of next 2tr, 1dc in next ch, 5ch, 1tr in 4ch sp, 5ch; repeat from ★ close with sl st.
6th rnd: ★ 1tr in each of next 4dc, 6ch, 1dbl tr in tr, 6ch; repeat from ★ close with sl st.
7th rnd: sl st into 2nd tr, ★ 2tr, 7ch, in dbl tr work (1dbl tr, 3ch) twice and 1dbl tr, 7ch; repeat from ★ close with sl st.
8th rnd: ★ 1tr in each of next 2tr, 7ch, (1dbl tr in dbl tr, 5ch) twice, 1dbl tr in next dbl tr, 7ch; repeat from ★ close with sl st.
9th rnd: ★1dc in each of next 2tr, 7dc in 7ch lp, 6dc in each 5ch lp, 7dc in 7ch lp; repeat from ★ close with sl st.

10th rnd: sl st over 2dc, ★ 1tr (1ch, skip 1dc, 1tr) 4 times, 4ch, in dc above centre dbl tr work 1tr 7ch 1tr, skip 3dc; repeat from ★ close with sl st.
11th rnd: ★ 1dc in each sp and tr, 2dbl tr cl in 7ch lp, in same 7ch lp work (6ch, 3dbl tr cl) 4 times and 6ch and 2dbl tr cl, 1dc in each sp and tr; repeat from ★ close with sl st.
12th rnd: ★ 1dc in the 2nd to 7th dc, in each of next five 7ch lps work (1tr, 2ch) 4 times and 1tr, 1dc in the 2nd to 7th dc; repeat from ★ close with sl st.
13th rnd: ★ 5dc, 1dc in 2ch sp, (3ch, 1dc, 2ch, 1dc) 9 times, 3ch, 5dc; repeat from ★ close with sl st.
14th rnd: 4ch (for first dbl tr), ★ 1ch, 1tr in first 3ch sp, 1ch, (skip 1sp, 1tr 5ch 1tr in next sp, 1ch) 8 times, 1tr in next 3ch sp, skip 5dc, 1dbl tr, 1ch; repeat from ★ close with sl st in 4th of 5ch.
15th rnd: sl st to centre of 5ch lp, ★ (2tr tr cl, 8ch) 7 times, 2tr tr cl; repeat from ★ close with sl st.
16th rnd: sl st to centre of 8ch lp, 1tr in same lp, ★ 4ch, in each of next 5 lps work (1tr, 3ch) twice and 1tr, 4ch, (1tr in centre of next lp) twice; repeat from ★ close with sl st.
17th rnd: ★ 4dc in 4ch sp, over three tr and sps work (1tr, 1p) twice, repeat from ★ close with sl st.
Fasten off.

Shamrock

Sandwich tray doily, 33 cm x 14 cm (13" x 5½")

Materials: 1 x 20g ball DMC No 40
piece of linen, 15 cm x 12 cm (6" x 4¾")
crochet hook No 0.75

Hand sew a narrow hem all around linen.
Work 8 lps of 15ch along each long side of linen, and lay linen aside.

Semi-circular pieces (make 2)
Commence with 10ch, close with sl st to form a ring.
1st row: 3ch, 13tr in ring, 7ch, turn.
2nd row: 1tr tr in each tr having 2ch between each, 2ch, 1tr tr in top of turning ch, 3ch, turn.
3rd row: 2tr in each sp, 1tr in each tr tr, ending with 1tr in 5th of turning ch, 5ch, turn.
4th row: (skip 1tr, 1tr in next tr, 2ch) 3 times, (skip 1tr, 1dbl tr in next tr, 2ch) twice, (skip 1tr, 1tr tr in next tr, 2ch) 8 times, (skip 1tr, 1dbl tr in next tr, 2ch) twice, (skip 1tr, 1tr in next tr, 2ch) 3 times, 1tr in top of turning ch, 3ch, turn (19 sps made).
5th row: (2tr in next sp, 1tr in next st) 4 times,

(2dbl tr in next sp, 1dbl tr in next st) twice, (3dbl tr in next sp, 1dbl tr in next st) 7 times, (2dbl tr in next sp, 1dbl tr in next st) twice, (2tr in next sp, 1tr in next st) 4 times, 5ch, turn.
6th row: skip first st, ★ 1dc in next st, 5ch, skip 2sts; repeat from ★ ending with 2ch, 1tr in top of turning ch, 10ch, turn (20 lps).
7th row: 3tr tr in each of next 2 lps leaving the last lp of each on hook, yoh and pull through all lps (cluster made), 7ch, 1dc in next lp, 7ch; repeat from ★ ending with 10ch, 1sl st in last lp (7 clusters made).
Fasten off.

Shamrocks (make 5)
Commence with 7ch, close with sl st to form a ring.
1st row: in ring work 10dc, close with sl st in first dc.
2nd row: (15ch, skip 3dc, 1dc in next dc) 3 times, 5ch, sl st in tip of first cluster of semi-circular piece, 1dc in each of last 5ch (this is the stem of shamrock), 25dc in each of 3 lps, close with sl st.
Fasten off.
Join stem of second shamrock to tip of 3rd cluster.
Make two more shamrocks like this, joining stem of one to tip of 5th cluster and stem of the other to tip of 7th cluster. Now work a 5th shamrock as before and join stem to tip of centre cluster.
Tack centre of straight edge of work to short end of linen. Sew straight edge of crocheted piece to linen edge as far as 5th lp.
Crochet another semi-circular piece and shamrocks to match and sew to opposite end of linen.
Attach thread to first 15ch lp on one long side of linen, in each lp work 5dc, 5ch, 1dc in 5th ch from hook (picot made), (2dc in same lp, 1p) 4 times, 5dc in same lp.
Now work along outer edge of crocheted parts as follows:

skip 15dc on first petal of shamrock, 1dc in next dc, 1p, (1dc in each of next 2dc, 1p) twice, 1dc in each of next 5dc of same petal, skip 1dc on next petal, 1dc in next petal, 1dc in each of next 2dc, 2ch, 1sl st in last picot of previous petal, 2ch, and complete picot as each of next 5dc, (1p, 1dc in each of next 2dc) 6 times, 1p, 1dc in next 5dc, 1dc in each of first 5dc of next petal, (1p, 1dc in each of next 2dc) 3 times, 3ch, 1tr in tip of next cluster, 3ch, 1dc in 13th dc of before, (1dc in each of next 2dc, 1p) twice, 1dc in each of next 5dc.

Work over next 2 petals as before, 5ch, 1dbl tr in tip of next cluster, 5ch.

Work over the 3 petals of next shamrocks as before, joining corresponding picots, 5ch, 1dbl tr in tip of centre cluster, 5ch.

Work over remaining 2 shamrocks to correspond with first 2, joining corresponding picots as before.

Now work over loops along linen edge and along petals of other crocheted part as before. Close with sl st.

Fasten off.

TABLE CLOTHS

Simplicity

78cm (31") circular supper cloth

Materials: 3 x 50g balls DMC No 20
                 crochet hook No 1.25
Note: In this pattern 1grp is: 2tr, 2ch, 2tr.

Commence with 10ch, close with sl st to form a
ring.
1st rnd: 3ch (for first tr), 19tr, close with sl st.
2nd rnd: ★ 1tr, 1ch; repeat from ★ close with
sl st.
3rd rnd: sl st to 1ch lp ★ 2tr 2ch 2tr in each 1ch sp,
skip 1sp; repeat from ★ close with sl st (10 grps
made).
4th rnd: sl st into 2ch sp, 2tr 2ch 2tr in each sp, ★
1ch, 2tr 2ch 2tr in next sp; repeat from ★ to end of rnd
ending with 1ch, close with sl st.
5th rnd: sl st into 2ch sp, 2tr 2ch 2tr in same sp, 2ch,
★ 2tr 2ch 2tr in next sp, 2ch; repeat from ★ close with
sl st.
6th rnd: sl st into sp, 2tr 2ch 2tr in same sp, 3ch, ★ 2tr
2ch 2tr in next sp, 3ch; repeat from ★ close with sl st.
7th rnd: sl st into sp, 1dc in same sp, ★ 11ch, turn,
skip 3ch, 5tr, 3ch, 1dc in same sp as last dc, sl st over
2tr, 2dc, 11ch, turn, skip 3ch, 5tr, 3ch, 2dc in same sp,
sl st over 2tr, 1dc in next sp; repeat from ★ close with
sl st (20 ladders made). Break off yarn.
8th rnd: attach thread to top of any ladder, 2dc 1ch
2dc in the 3ch sp at the top of each ladder, divided by
4ch.
9th rnd: ★ 2tr 2ch 2tr grp in 1ch sp, 2tr 2ch 2tr in
centre of 4ch sp; repeat from ★ close with sl st
(40 grps made).
10th rnd: sl st into 2ch sp, ★ 1grp in each 2ch sp,
divided by 1ch; repeat from ★ close with sl st.
11th and 12th rnds: as 10th rnd.
13th rnd: sl st into 2ch sp, ★ 1grp in each 2ch sp
divided by 2ch; repeat from ★ close with sl st.
14th and 15th rnds: as 13th rnd.
16th rnd: sl st into 2ch sp, ★ 1grp in each 2ch sp
divided by 3ch; repeat from ★ close with sl st.
17th and 18th rnds: as 16th rnd.
19th rnd: 2tr in first grp, ★ 6ch, 2tr 2ch 2tr in next grp,
6ch, 2tr in next grp; repeat from ★ close with sl st.

20th rnd: 3ch (for first tr), 2tr, 5ch, 1grp, 5ch, ★ 4tr,
5ch, 1grp, 5ch; repeat from ★ ending with 1tr, close
with sl st.
21st to 25th rnds: continue this way, increasing 1tr at
each side of diamond and decreasing 1ch between
diamonds and grps till diamond is 14tr wide and no
chain stitch between.
26th rnd: 12tr on each diamond with 2ch between.
27th rnd: 10tr on each diamond with 3ch between.
28th rnd: 8tr on each diamond with 5ch between.
29th rnd: 6tr on each diamond with 7ch between.
30th rnd: 4tr on each diamond with 8ch between.
31st rnd: 2tr on each diamond with 9ch between.
32nd rnd: ★ 2tr in first tr, 2ch, 2tr in next tr, 10ch, 2tr
in grp; repeat from ★ close with sl st.
33rd rnd: sl st into grp, ★ 1grp, 9ch, 4tr, 9ch; repeat
from ★ close with sl st.
34th rnd: as 33rd rnd but with 6tr on diamond.
35th rnd: sl st into grp, ★ 1grp, 8ch, 8tr, 8ch; repeat
from ★ close with sl st.
36th rnd: sl st into grp, ★ 1grp, 7ch, 10tr, 7ch; repeat
from ★ close with sl st.
37th rnd: sl st into grp, ★ 1grp, 6ch, 12tr, 6ch; repeat
from ★ close with sl st.
38th rnd: sl st into grp, ★ 1grp, 5ch, 14tr, 5ch; repeat
from ★ close with sl st.

39th rnd: as 38th rnd but with 16tr on diamond.

40th rnd: sl st into grp, ★ 1grp, 4ch, 18tr, 4ch; repeat from ★ close with sl st.

41st rnd: sl st into grp, ★ in grp work (2tr 2ch) twice and 2tr, 4ch, skip first and last tr and work 16tr on diamond, 4ch; repeat from ★ close with sl st.

42nd rnd: sl st into grp, ★ 1grp, 1ch, 1grp, 3ch, 16tr, 3ch; repeat from ★ close with sl st.

43rd rnd: sl st into grp, ★ 1grp, 3ch, 1grp, 3ch, 1grp, 3ch, 14tr, 3ch; repeat from ★ close with sl st.

44th rnd: sl st into grp, ★ 1grp, 5ch, 1grp, 3ch, 14tr, 3ch; repeat from ★ close with sl st.

45th rnd: sl st into grp, ★ 1grp, 3ch, 2tr in centre of 5ch lp, 3ch, 1grp, 3ch, 12tr, 3ch; repeat from ★ close with sl st.

46th rnd: sl st into grp, ★ 1grp, 3ch, 2tr in first tr, 2ch, 2tr in next tr, 3ch, 1grp, 3ch, 12tr, 3ch; repeat from ★ close with sl st.

47th rnd: sl st into grp, ★ (1grp, 5ch) twice, 1grp, 3ch, 10tr, 3ch; repeat from ★ close with sl st.

48th rnd: sl st into grp, ★ 1grp, 3ch, 2tr in centre of 5ch lop, 3ch, 1grp, 3ch, 2tr in centre of next 5ch lp, 3ch, 1grp, 3ch, 10tr, 3ch; repeat from ★ close with sl st.

49th rnd: sl st into grp, ★ (1grp, 3ch) 4 times, 1grp, 3ch, 8tr, 3ch; repeat from ★ close with sl st.

50th rnd: as 49th rnd.

51st rnd: sl st into grp, ★ (1grp, 5ch) 4 times, 1grp, 3ch, 6tr, 3ch; repeat from ★ close with sl st.

52nd rnd: sl st into grp, ★ (1grp, 6ch) 4 times, 1grp, 3ch, 6tr, 3ch; repeat from ★ close with sl st.

53rd rnd: sl st into grp, ★ (1grp, 3ch, 2tr in centre of 5ch lp, 3ch) 4 times, 3ch, 4tr, 3ch; repeat from ★ close with sl st.

54th rnd: sl st into grp, ★ (1grp, 1ch) 8 times, 1grp, 3ch, 4tr, 3ch; repeat from ★ close with sl st.

55th rnd: sl st into grp, ★ (1grp, 1ch) 8 times, 1grp, 2ch, 2tr, 2ch; repeat from ★ close with sl st.

56th rnd: sl st into grp, ★ (1grp, 2ch) 8 times, 1grp, 2ch, skip 2tr; repeat from ★ close with sl st.

57th rnd: sl st into grp, 2tr in same grp, 2ch, ★ (1grp, 2ch) 7 times, 2tr in each of next 2grps, 2ch; repeat from ★ close with sl st.

58th rnd: sl st into grp, ★ (1grp, 3ch) 7 times, 2tr in centre of next 4tr, 3ch; repeat from ★ close with sl st.

59th rnd: sl st into grp, ★ (1grp, 3ch) 6 times, 1grp, 2ch, 2tr, 2ch; repeat from ★ close with sl st.

60th rnd: sl st into grp, ★ (1grp, 5ch) 6 times, 1grp, skip 2tr; repeat from ★ close with sl st.

61st rnd: sl st into grp, 2tr, ★ 4ch, (1grp, 6ch) 4 times, 1grp, 4ch, 2tr in each of next 2 grps; repeat from ★ ending with 2tr in last grp.

62nd rnd: sl st into next grp, ★ (1grp, 3ch, 2tr in centre of next 6ch 1p, 3ch) 4 times, 1grp, 4ch, 1dc between 4tr, 4ch; repeat from ★ close with sl st.

63rd rnd: sl st into grp, ★ (1grp 1ch 1grp in 2tr, 1ch) 4 times, 1grp, 3ch, 1dc, 3ch; repeat from ★ close with sl st.

64th rnd: sl st into grp, ★ (2tr, 4ch, 1dc in base of 4ch (picot made), 2tr in grp, 2ch) 8 times, 2tr 1p 2tr in next grp, 2ch, 1dc in dc, 2ch; repeat from ★ close with sl st.

Fasten off.

Waves

53 cm (21") circular coffee cloth

Materials: 2 x 20g balls DMC No 40
crochet hook No 0.75

Commence with 6ch, close with sl st to form a ring.
1st rnd: 3ch, 15tr in ring, close with sl st.
2nd rnd: 5ch, ★ 1tr in next tr, 2ch; repeat from ★ close with sl st in 3rd of 5ch (16 spaces made).
3rd rnd: 6ch, ★ 1tr in next tr, 3ch; repeat from ★ close with sl st in 3rd of 6ch.
4th rnd: 7ch, ★ 1tr in next tr, 4ch; repeat from ★ close with sl st in 3rd of 7ch.
5th rnd: 10ch, ★ 1tr in next tr, 7ch; repeat from ★ close with sl st in 3rd of 10ch.
6th rnd: sl st into 7ch sp, 3ch, 8tr in same sp, 9tr in each of remaining 15sps, close with sl st.
7th rnd: 3ch, 1tr in next tr, ★ 5ch, skip 1tr, 1dbl tr in next tr, 1ch, skip 1tr, 1dbl tr in next tr, 5ch, skip 1tr, 1tr in each of next 13tr; repeat from ★ ending with 11tr instead of 13tr at end of last repeat, close with sl st.
8th rnd: sl st over next tr and 2ch, 1tr in next ch, ★ 5ch, 1dbl tr in next dbl tr, 1ch, 1dbl tr in next dbl tr, 5ch (skip 1ch, 1tr in next ch) twice, 1ch, skip 1ch and 2tr, 1tr in each of next 9tr, 1ch, skip 2tr and 1ch, 1tr in next ch, 1ch, skip 1ch, 1tr in next ch; repeat from ★ omitting 2tr with 1ch between at end of last repeat, close with sl st.
9th rnd: 4ch, 1tr in next tr, ★ (1ch, skip 1ch, 1tr in next ch) twice, 5ch, 1dbl tr in next dbl tr, 1ch, 1dbl tr in next dbl tr, 5ch, (skip 1ch, 1tr in next ch, 1ch) twice, (1tr in next tr, 1ch) twice, skip 1ch and 2tr, 1tr in each of next 5tr, 1ch, skip 2tr and 1ch, 1tr in next tr, 1ch, 1tr in next tr; repeat from ★ omitting 2tr with 1ch between at end of last repeat, close with sl st in 3rd of 4ch.
10th rnd: 4ch, ★ (1tr in next tr, 1ch) 3 times, skip 1ch, 1tr in next ch, 1ch, skip 1ch, 1tr in next ch, 5ch, 1dbl tr in next dbl tr, 1ch, 1dbl tr in next dbl tr, 5ch, skip 1ch, 1tr in next ch, 1ch, skip 1ch, 1tr in next ch, (1ch, 1tr in next tr) 4 times, 1ch, skip 1ch and 1tr, 1tr in each of next 3tr, 1ch, skip 1tr and 1ch, 1tr in next tr, 1ch; repeat from ★ omitting 1tr and 1ch at end of last repeat, close with sl st in 3rd of 4ch.
11th rnd: 4ch, ★ (1tr in next tr, 1ch) 5 times, skip 1ch, 1tr in next ch, 1ch, skip 1ch, 1tr in next ch, 5ch, 1dbl tr in next dbl tr, 1ch, 1dbl tr in next dbl tr, 5ch, skip 1ch, 1tr in next ch, 1ch, skip 1ch, 1tr in next ch, (1ch, 1tr in next tr) 6 times, 1ch, 3tr cl, 1ch, 1tr in next tr, 1ch; repeat from ★ omitting 1tr and 1ch at end of last repeat, close with sl st in 3rd of 4ch.
12th rnd: 4ch, 1tr in next tr, 1ch, 1tr in next tr, 13ch, 1sl st in 1st of 13ch, ★ 1tr in next tr, (1ch, 1tr in next tr) twice, 9ch, 1sl st in 1st of 9ch, (1tr in next tr, 1ch) twice, (skip 1ch, 1tr in next ch, 1ch) twice, (1tr in next dbl tr, 1ch) twice, (skip 1ch, 1tr in next ch, 1ch)

twice, 1tr in next tr, 1ch, 1tr in next tr, 9ch, 1sl st in 1st of 9ch, (1tr in next tr, 1ch) twice, 1tr in next tr, 13ch, 1sl st in 1st of 13ch, 1tr in next tr, 1ch, 1tr in next tr, 1ch, 1tr in next tr, skip cluster, (1tr in next tr, 1ch) twice, 1tr in next tr, 7ch, 1sl st in last 13ch lp, 6ch, 1sl st in 1st of 7ch; repeat from ★ 6 more times, (1tr in next tr, 1ch) twice, 1tr in next tr, 9ch, 1sl st in 1st of 9ch, (1tr in next tr, 1ch) twice, skip 1ch, 1tr in next ch, 1ch, skip 1ch, 1tr in next ch, 1ch, (1tr in next dbl tr, 1ch) twice, (skip 1ch, 1tr in next ch, 1ch) twice, 1tr in next tr, 1ch, 1tr in next tr, 9ch, 1sl st in 1st of 9ch, (1tr in next tr, 1ch) twice, 1tr in next tr, 7ch, 1sl st in first lp of 13ch, 6ch, 1sl st in first of 7ch, (1tr in next tr, 1ch) twice, 1tr in next tr, close with sl st 3rd of 4ch.
Break off yarn.
13th rnd: Join yarn in first 9ch lp of previous rnd, 8ch, 1tr in same lp, ★ 4ch 1dbl tr in same lp, 6ch, skip 4sps, 1dc in next sp, 6ch, in next 9ch lp work 1dbl tr 4ch 1tr 4ch and 1dbl tr, 6ch, 1dbl tr in sl st at join of next 2lps, 6ch, 1dbl tr in next 9ch lp, 4ch, 1tr in same lp; repeat from ★ omitting 1dbl tr, 4ch, 1tr at end of last repeat, close with sl st in 4th of 8ch.
14th rnd: 3ch, ★ 4tr in 4ch sp, 4tr in next 4ch sp, 1tr in dbl tr, 1tr in next 6ch sp, 5ch, 1sl st in top of last tr (picot made), 5tr in same 6ch sp, 6tr in next 6ch sp, 1p, 1tr in next dbl tr; repeat from ★ omitting tr at end of last repeat, close with sl st.
15th rnd: sl st over next 10tr and into picot, 1dc in same picot, ★ 11ch, 1dc in next picot; repeat from ★ ending with 11ch, close with sl st in first dc (32 loops made).
16th rnd: sl st in 11ch lp, 3ch, 10tr in same lp, 11tr in each 11ch lps, close with sl st.
17th rnd: 3ch, 1tr in next tr, ★ 5ch, skip 2tr, 1dbl tr in next tr, 1ch, skip 1tr, 1dbl tr in next tr, 5ch, skip 2tr, 5ch, skip 2tr, 1tr in each of next 15tr; repeat from ★ ending with 13tr instead of 15tr at end of last repeat, close with sl st.
18th rnd: as 8th rnd, having 11tr instead of 9tr in tr grps.
19th rnd: as 9th rnd, having 7tr instead of 5tr in tr grps.
20th rnd: as 10th rnd, skipping 2tr instead of 1tr before and after 3tr grps.
21st rnd: as 11th rnd.
22nd rnd: as 12th rnd, having 14 repeats instead of 6.
Break off yarn.
Note: 23rd and 24th rnds take some concentration.
23rd rnd: join yarn in first 9ch lp of previous rnd, 7ch, 1tr in same lp, ★ 9ch, 1sl st in top of last tr, 3ch, 1dbl tr in same lp, 4ch, skip 4sps, 1dc in next sp, 9ch, 1sl st in last dc, 4ch, 1dbl tr in next 9ch lp, 3ch, 1tr in same lp, 9ch, 1sl st in top of last tr, 3ch, 1dbl tr in same lp, 4ch, 1dbl tr in sl st at join of next 2lps, 9ch,

1sl st in top of dbl tr, 4ch, 1dbl tr in next 9ch lp, 3ch, 1tr in same lp; repeat from * omitting 1dbl tr, 3ch 1tr at end of last repeat, close with sl st in 4th of 7ch.

24th rnd: sl st over next 3ch, 1sl st in tr, sl st to centre of 9ch lp, 1dc in same lp, 12ch, sl st in 3rd of 12ch, * 4ch, 1tr tr in same lp leaving last lp on hook, 1tr in 9ch lp leaving last lp on hook, yoh, pull through all lps on hook, 5ch, sl st in top of tr tr, 4ch, 1tr in same lp as last tr tr, 9ch 1sl st in top of last tr; repeat from * omitting 1tr and 9ch lp at end of last repeat, close with sl st in 3rd of 12ch.

25th rnd: sl st to centre of 9ch lp and continue as 24th rnd.

Repeat 25th rnd twice more.

28th rnd: sl st to centre of 9ch lp, 1dc in same lp, 7ch, 1tr in same lp, 3ch, 1dbl tr in same lp, * 3ch, in next 9ch lp work 1dbl tr 3ch 1tr 3ch and 1dbl tr; repeat from * ending with 3ch, close with sl st in 4th of 7ch.

29th rnd: 3ch (for first tr), continue rnd working 3tr in each space of 3ch, and 1tr in each dbl tr, working a picot (5ch, 1sl st in top of last tr) above 8th tr and each of 9th tr respectively, ending with 8tr, 1p, (10tr, 1p) twice, close with sl st (78 picots, or number divisible by 3).

30th rnd: sl st over next 7tr, sl st to top of picot, 1dc in picot, * 11ch, 1dc in next picot; repeat from * ending with 11ch, close with sl st in first dc.

31st rnd: sl st in 11ch lp, 3ch, 8tr in same lp, 9tr in each 11ch lp, 3ch; close with sl st.

32nd rnd: 3ch, 1tr in each of next 17tr, * 5ch, skip 3tr, 1dbl tr in next tr, 1ch, skip 1tr, 1dbl tr in next tr, 5ch, skip 3tr, 1tr in each of next 18tr; repeat from * omitting 18tr at end of last repeat, close with sl st.

33rd rnd: sl st over next 2tr, 3ch, 1tr in each of next 13tr, * 1ch, skip 2tr and 1ch, 1tr in next ch, 1ch, skip 1ch, 1tr in next ch, 5ch, 1dbl tr in next dbl tr, 1ch, 1dbl tr in next dbl tr, 5ch, skip 1ch, 1tr in next ch, 1ch, skip 1ch, 1tr in next ch, 1ch, skip 1ch and 2tr, 1tr in each of next 14tr; repeat from * omitting 14tr at end of last repeat, close with sl st.

34th rnd: sl st over next 2tr, 3ch, 1tr in each of next 9tr, * 1ch, skip 2tr and 1ch, (1tr in next tr, 1ch) twice, skip 1ch, 1tr in next ch, 1ch, skip 1ch, 1tr in next ch, 5ch, 1dbl tr in next dbl tr, 1ch, 1dbl tr in next dbl tr, 5ch, (skip 1ch, 1tr in next ch, 1ch) twice, (1tr in next tr, 1ch) twice, skip 1ch and 2tr, 1tr in each of next 10tr; repeat from * omitting 10tr at end of last repeat, close with sl st.

35th rnd: sl st over next 2tr, 3ch, 1tr in each of next 5tr, * (1ch, skip 2tr and 1ch, 1tr in next tr, 1ch) 4 times, (1ch, 1tr in next ch) twice, 5ch, 1dbl tr in next dbl tr, 1ch, 1dbl tr in next dbl tr, 5ch, (skip 1ch, 1tr in next ch) twice, (1ch, 1tr in next tr) 4 times,

1ch, skip 1ch and 2tr, 1tr in each of next 6tr; repeat from * omitting 6tr at end of last repeat, close with sl st.

36th rnd: sl st in next tr, 3ch, 3tr cl, * 1ch, skip 1tr and 1ch, (1tr in next tr, 1ch) 6 times, (skip 1ch, 1tr in next ch) twice, 5ch, 1dbl tr in next dbl tr, 1ch, 1dbl tr in next dbl tr, 5ch, skip 1ch, 1tr in next ch, 1ch, skip 1ch, 1tr in next ch, (1ch, 1tr in next tr) 6 times, 1ch, skip 1ch and 1tr, 4tr cl; repeat from * omitting cluster at end of last repeat, close with sl st in top of first cluster.

37th rnd: sl st over next ch and tr, 8ch, 1sl st in 3rd of 8ch, * (1tr in next tr, 1ch, 1tr in next tr, 5ch, sl st in first of 5ch [picot made]) 3 times, 1tr in next tr, 1ch, skip 1ch, 1tr in next ch, 1p, skip 1ch, 1tr in next ch, 1ch, 1tr in dbl tr, 1p, 1tr in next dbl tr, 1ch, skip 1ch, 1tr in next ch, 1p, skip 1ch, 1tr in next ch, (1ch, 1tr in next tr, 1p) 4 times, 1tr in next tr, skip cluster, 1tr in next tr, 1p; repeat from * omitting picot at end of last repeat, close with sl st in 3rd of 8ch.

Fasten off.

Autumn Leaves

56 cm (22") circular coffee cloth

This beautiful coffee cloth is well worth the extra concentration it will take to make it, and is for the more experienced crocheter. The design consists entirely of double treble and chain stitches.

Materials: 4 x 20g balls DMC No 40
crochet hook No 0.75

Note: Commence each rnd with 4ch for first double treble.

Commence with 8ch, close with sl st to form a ring.
1st rnd: 4ch (for first dbl tr), 3dbl tr cl, (4ch, 4dbl tr cl) 5 times, 4ch (6dbl tr clusters made).
2nd rnd: in each 5ch lp work 4dbl tr cl 4ch 4dbl tr cl, divided by 3ch, close with sl st.
3rd rnd: sl st into 4ch sp, * 4dbl tr cl 4ch 4dbl tr cl in same 4ch sp, 3ch, 1dbl tr in same place as last cl, 1dbl tr in next 4ch sp, 3ch, 4dbl tr cl 4ch 4dbl tr cl in same 4ch sp, 3ch, 1dbl tr in same 4ch sp, 1dbl tr in next 4ch sp; repeat from * ending with 3ch, close with sl st.
4th rnd: sl st into 4ch sp, * 4dbl tr cl 4ch 4dbl tr cl in 4ch sp, 3ch, 1dbl tr in same sp as last cl, 1dbl tr in dbl tr, 3ch, 1dbl tr in same dbl tr, 1dbl tr in next 4ch sp, 3ch; repeat from * close with sl st.
5th rnd: sl st into 4ch sp, * 4dbl tr cl 4ch 4dbl tr cl

Waves coffee cloth (page 22)

Autumn Leaves coffee cloth (page 24)

Starflower doily (page 16)

Aster doily (page 16)

Above: Potpourri doily (page 18)   Below: Tulip doily (page 17)

in 4ch sp, 3ch, 1dbl tr in same sp as last cl, (1dbl tr
in next dbl tr, 3ch, 1dbl tr in same place as last
dbl tr) twice, 1dbl tr in next 4ch sp, 3ch; repeat
from ★ close with sl st.

6th rnd: sl st into 4ch sp, ★ 4dbl tr cl 4ch 4dbl tr cl
in 4ch sp, 3ch, 1dbl tr in same place as last cl, 1dbl tr
3ch 1dbl tr in next dbl tr, 3dbl tr in next dbl tr,
1dbl tr 3ch 1dbl tr in next dbl tr, 1dbl tr in next
4ch sp, 3ch; repeat from ★ close with sl st.

7th rnd: sl st into 4ch sp, ★ 4dbl tr cl 4ch 4dbl tr cl
in 4ch sp, 1dbl tr in same place as last cl, 1dbl tr 3ch
1dbl tr in next dbl tr, skip 3ch, 2dbl tr 2ch in each of
next 2dbl tr, 2dbl tr in third dbl tr, 1dbl tr 3ch
1dbl tr in next dbl tr, skip 3ch, 1dbl tr in next
4ch sp, 3ch; repeat from ★ close with sl st.

8th rnd: sl st into 4ch sp, ★ 4dbl tr cl 4ch 4dbl tr cl
in 4ch sp, 3ch, 1dbl tr in same place as last cl, 1dbl tr
3ch 1dbl tr in next dbl tr, (3dbl tr in next dbl tr
2ch) twice, 2dbl tr, (2ch 3dbl tr in next dbl tr) twice,
1dbl tr 3ch 1dbl tr in next dbl tr, 1dbl tr in next
4ch sp, 3ch; repeat from ★ close with sl st.

9th rnd: sl st into 4ch sp, ★ 4dbl tr cl 4ch 4dbl tr cl
in 4ch sp, 3ch, 1dbl tr in same place as last cl, 1dbl tr
3ch 1dbl tr in next dbl tr, (2dbl tr in next

dbl tr, 1dbl tr, 2dbl tr in next dbl tr, 2ch) twice,
2dbl tr, (2ch, 2dbl tr in next dbl tr, 1dbl tr, 2dbl tr
in next dbl tr) twice, 1dbl tr 3ch 1dbl tr in next
dbl tr, 1dbl tr in next 4ch sp, 3ch; repeat from ★
close with sl st.

10th rnd: sl st into 4ch sp, ★ 4dbl tr cl 4ch
4dbl tr cl in 4ch sp, 3ch, 1dbl tr in same place as last
cl, 1dbl tr 3ch 1dbl tr in next dbl tr, (5dbl tr, 2ch)
twice, 3dbl tr in 2dbl tr, (2ch, 5dbl tr) twice, 1dbl tr
3ch 1dbl tr in next dbl tr, 1dbl tr in next 4ch sp,
3ch; repeat from ★ close with sl st.

11th rnd: sl st into 4ch sp, ★ 4dbl tr cl 5ch
4dbl tr cl in same 4ch sp, 3ch, 1dbl tr in same place
as last cl, 1dbl tr 3ch 1dbl tr in next dbl tr,
2dbl tr cl, 3dbl tr, skip 2ch, 2dbl tr cl, 3dbl tr, 2ch,
(2dbl tr in next dbl tr, 2ch) twice, 2dbl tr in next
dbl tr, 2ch, 2dbl tr cl, 3dbl tr, skip 2ch, 2dbl tr cl,
3dbl tr, 1dbl tr 3ch 1dbl tr in next dbl tr, 1dbl tr in
next 4ch sp, 3ch; repeat from ★ close with sl st.

12th rnd: sl st into 5ch sp, ★ in same 5ch sp work
(4dbl tr cl 4ch 4dbl tr cl) 3 times and 4dbl tr cl,
1dbl tr 3ch 1dbl tr in next dbl tr, skip 3ch, 1dbl tr in
next dbl tr, 3ch, 2dbl tr cl, 4dbl tr, 2dbl tr cl, 2ch,
(3dbl tr in next dbl tr, 2ch) twice, 2dbl tr, (2ch,

29

3dbl tr in next dbl tr) twice, 2ch, 2dbl tr cl, 4dbl tr, 2dbl tr cl, 3ch, 1dbl tr in same place as last cl, 1dbl tr 3ch 1dbl tr in next dbl tr; repeat from ★ close with sl st.

13th rnd: sl st into 4ch sp, ★ 4dbl tr cl 4ch 4dbl tr cl between each dbl tr grp divided by 3ch (3dbl tr grps made), 1dbl tr 3ch 1dbl tr in next dbl tr, 1dbl tr in next dbl tr, 3ch, 6dbl tr cl, 1ch, (2dbl tr in next dbl tr, 1dbl tr, 2dbl tr in next dbl tr, 2ch) twice, 2dbl tr, (2ch, 2dbl tr in next dbl tr, 1dbl tr, 2dbl tr in next dbl tr) twice, 1ch, 6dbl tr cl, 3ch, 1dbl tr in same place as last cl, 1dbl tr 3ch 1dbl tr in next dbl tr; repeat from ★ close with sl st.

14th rnd: sl st into 4ch sp, ★ (4dbl tr cl 4ch 4dbl tr cl in 4ch sp, 3ch, 1dbl tr in same 4ch sp, 1dbl tr in next 4ch sp, 3ch) twice, 4dbl tr cl 4ch 4dbl tr cl in next 4ch sp, 1dbl tr 3ch 1dbl tr in next dbl tr, 1dbl tr 3ch 1dbl tr in 6dbl tr cl, (5dbl tr 2ch) twice, (3dbl tr in next dbl tr, 2ch) twice, 5dbl tr, 2ch, 5dbl tr, 1dbl tr 3ch 1dbl tr in 6dbl tr cl, 1dbl tr 3ch 1dbl tr in next dbl tr; repeat from ★ close with sl st.

15th rnd: sl st into 4ch sp, ★ (4dbl tr cl 4ch 4dbl tr cl in 4ch sp, 3ch, 1dbl tr in same place as last cl, 1dbl tr 3ch 1dbl tr in next dbl tr, 1dbl tr in next 4ch sp, 3ch) twice, 4dbl tr cl 4ch 4dbl tr cl in next 4ch sp, 1dbl tr 3ch 1dbl tr in next dbl tr, 1dbl tr in next dbl tr, 3ch, 2dbl tr cl, 3dbl tr, skip 2ch, 2dbl tr, 2dbl tr cl, (2ch, 2dbl tr in next dbl tr, 1dbl tr, 2dbl tr in next dbl tr) twice, 2ch, 2dbl tr cl in next dbl tr, 3dbl tr, skip 2ch, 3dbl tr, 2dbl tr cl, 3ch, 1dbl tr in same place as last cl, 1dbl tr 3ch 1dbl tr in next dbl tr; repeat from ★ close with sl st.

16th rnd: sl st into 4ch sp, ★ (4dbl tr cl 4ch 4dbl tr cl in 4ch sp, 3ch, 1dbl tr in same place as last cl, [1dbl tr 3ch 1dbl tr in next dbl tr] twice, 1dbl tr in next 4ch sp, 3ch) twice, 4dbl tr cl 4ch 4dbl tr cl in next 4ch sp, 1dbl tr 3ch 1dbl tr in next dbl tr, 1dbl tr in next dbl tr, 3ch, 2dbl tr cl 4dbl tr 2dbl tr cl (2ch, 5dbl tr) twice, 2ch, 2dbl tr in next dbl tr, 4dbl tr, 2dbl tr cl in next dbl tr, 3ch, 1dbl tr in same place as last 2dbl tr cl, 1dbl tr 3ch 1dbl tr in next dbl tr; repeat from ★ close with sl st.

17th rnd: sl st into 4ch sp, ★ (4dbl tr cl 4ch 4dbl tr cl in 4ch sp, 3ch, 1dbl tr in same place as last cl, 1dbl tr 3ch 1dbl tr in next dbl tr, 3dbl tr in next dbl tr, 1dbl tr 3ch 1dbl tr in next dbl tr, 1dbl tr in next 4ch sp, 3ch) twice, 4dbl tr cl 4ch 4dbl tr cl in next 4ch sp, 1dbl tr 3ch 1dbl tr in next dbl tr, 1dbl tr in next dbl tr, 6dbl tr cl, 2ch, 2dbl tr cl, 3dbl tr, skip 2ch, 3dbl tr, 2dbl tr cl, 2ch, 6dbl tr cl, 3ch, 1dbl tr in same place as last cl, 1dbl tr 3ch 1dbl tr in next dbl tr; repeat from ★ close with sl st.

18th rnd: sl st into 4ch sp, ★ (4dbl tr cl 4ch 4dbl tr cl in 4ch sp, 3ch 1dbl tr 3ch 1dbl tr in next

dbl tr, [2dbl tr, 2ch] twice, 2dbl tr, 1dbl tr 3ch 1dbl tr in next dbl tr, 1dbl tr in next 4ch sp, 3ch) twice, 4dbl tr cl 4ch 4dbl tr cl in 4ch sp, 1dbl tr 3ch 1dbl tr in next dbl tr, 1dbl tr 3ch 1dbl tr in 6dbl tr cl, 2dbl tr cl, 4dbl tr, 2dbl tr cl, 1dbl tr 3ch 1dbl tr in 6dbl tr cl, 1dbl tr 3ch 1dbl tr in next dbl tr; repeat from ★ close with sl st.

19th rnd: sl st into 4ch sp, ★ (4dbl tr cl 4ch 4dbl tr cl in 4ch sp, 3ch, 1dbl tr in same place as last cl, 1dbl tr 3ch 1dbl tr in next dbl tr, [3dbl tr in next dbl tr, 2ch] twice, 2dbl tr [2ch, 3dbl tr in next dbl tr] twice, 1dbl tr 3ch 1dbl tr in next dbl tr, 1dbl tr in next 4ch sp, 3ch) twice, 4dbl tr cl 4ch 4dbl tr cl in 4ch sp, 1dbl tr 3ch 1dbl tr in next dbl tr, 1dbl tr in next dbl tr, 3ch, 6dbl tr cl, 3ch, 1dbl tr in same place as 6dbl tr cl, 1dbl tr 3ch 1dbl tr in next dbl tr; repeat from ★ close with sl st.

20th rnd: sl st into 4ch sp, ★ (4dbl tr cl 4ch 4dbl tr cl in 4ch sp, 3ch, 1dbl tr in same place as last cl, 1dbl tr 3ch 1dbl tr in next dbl tr, [2dbl tr in next dbl tr, 1dbl tr, 2dbl tr in next dbl tr, 2ch] twice, 2dbl tr, [2ch, 2dbl tr in next dbl tr, 1dbl tr, 2dbl tr in next dbl tr] twice, 1dbl tr 3ch 1dbl tr in next dbl tr, 1dbl tr in 4ch sp, 3ch) twice, 4dbl tr cl 4ch 4dbl tr cl in 4ch sp, 1dbl tr 3ch 1dbl tr in next dbl tr, 1dbl tr 3ch 1dbl tr in 6dbl tr cl, 1dbl tr 3ch 1dbl tr in next dbl tr; repeat from ★ close with sl st.

21st rnd: sl st into 4ch sp, ★ (4dbl tr cl 4ch 4dbl tr cl in 4ch sp, 3ch, 1dbl tr in same place as last cl, 1dbl tr 3ch 1dbl tr in next dbl tr, [5dbl tr, 2ch] twice, 3dbl tr in 2dbl tr, [2ch, 5dbl tr] twice, 1dbl tr 3ch 1dbl tr in next dbl tr, 1dbl tr in 4ch sp, 3ch) twice, 4dbl tr cl 4ch 4dbl tr cl in 4ch sp, (1dbl tr 3ch 1dbl tr in next dbl tr) twice; repeat from ★ close with sl st.

22nd rnd: sl st into 4ch sp, ★ (4dbl tr cl 5ch 4dbl tr cl in 4ch sp, 3ch, 1dbl tr in same place as last cl, 1dbl tr 3ch 1dbl tr in next dbl tr, 2dbl tr cl, 2dbl tr, skip 2ch, 2dbl tr, 2dbl tr cl, [2ch, 2dbl tr in next dbl tr] twice, 2dbl tr in next dbl tr, 2ch, 2dbl tr cl, 2dbl tr, skip 2ch, 2dbl tr, 2dbl tr cl in next dbl tr, 1dbl tr 3ch 1dbl tr in next dbl tr, 1dbl tr in next 4ch sp) twice, 4dbl tr cl 5ch 4dbl tr cl in 4ch sp, 1dbl tr in dbl tr; repeat from ★ close with sl st.

23rd rnd: sl st to centre of 5ch sp, 4dbl tr cl 4ch 4dbl tr cl in 5ch sp, ★ 1dbl tr 3ch 1dbl tr in next dbl tr, 1dbl tr in next dbl tr, 2dbl tr cl, 4dbl tr, 2dbl tr cl, 2ch, (3dbl tr in next dbl tr, 2ch) twice, 2dbl tr, (2ch, 2dbl tr in next dbl tr) twice, 2ch, 2dbl tr cl, 4dbl tr, 2dbl tr cl, 3ch, 1dbl tr in same place as last cl, 2dbl tr 3ch 1dbl tr in next dbl tr, (4dbl tr cl 4ch 4dbl tr cl) twice in next 5ch lp divided by 4ch; repeat from ★ ending with 4dbl tr cl 4ch 4dbl tr cl in same 5ch sp as first 4dbl tr cl, 4ch, close with sl st.

24th rnd: sl st into 4ch sp, 4dbl tr cl 4ch 4dbl tr cl in 4ch sp, ★ 1dbl tr 3ch 1dbl tr in next dbl tr, 1dbl tr in next dbl tr, 3ch, 6dbl tr cl, 2ch, 2dbl tr in next dbl tr, 3dbl tr, 2ch, 3dbl tr, 2dbl tr in next dbl tr, 2ch, 2dbl tr, 2ch, 2dbl tr in next dbl tr, 3dbl tr, 2ch, 3dbl tr, 2dbl tr in next dbl tr, 3ch, 6dbl tr cl, 3ch, 1dbl tr in same place as 6dbl tr cl, 1dbl tr 3ch 1dbl tr in next dbl tr, 4dbl tr cl 4ch 4dbl tr cl in each of next three 4ch lps divided by 4ch; repeat from ★ ending with 4dbl tr cl 4ch 4dbl tr cl in last two 4ch sps divided by 4ch, close with sl st.

25th rnd: sl st into 4ch sp, ★ 4dbl tr cl 4ch 4dbl tr cl in 4ch sp, 1dbl tr 3ch 1dbl tr in next dbl tr, 1dbl tr 3ch 1dbl tr in 6dbl tr cl, (5dbl tr, 2ch) twice, (3dbl tr in next dbl tr, 2ch) twice, 5dbl tr, 2ch, 5dbl tr, 1dbl tr 3ch 1dbl tr in 6dbl tr cl, 1dbl tr 3ch 1dbl tr in next dbl tr, (4dbl tr cl 4ch 4dbl tr cl in 4ch sp, 3ch, 1dbl tr in same place as last cl, 1dbl tr in 4ch sp, 3ch) twice; repeat from ★ close with sl st.

26th rnd: sl st into 4ch sp, ★ 4dbl tr cl 4ch 4dbl tr cl in 4ch sp, 1dbl tr 3ch 1dbl tr in dbl tr, 1dbl tr in next dbl tr, 3ch, 2dbl tr cl, 3dbl tr, skip 2ch, 3dbl tr, 2dbl tr cl, 2ch, (2dbl tr in next dbl tr, 1dbl tr, 2dbl tr in next dbl tr, 2ch) twice, 2dbl tr cl, 3dbl tr, 2dbl tr cl, skip 2ch, 2dbl tr cl, 3dbl tr, 2dbl tr cl, 3ch, 1dbl tr in same place as last dbl tr, 1dbl tr 3ch 1dbl tr in next dbl tr, (4dbl tr cl 4ch 4dbl tr cl in 4ch sp, 3ch, 1dbl tr in same place as last cl, 4dbl tr cl 4ch 4dbl tr cl in dbl tr, 1dbl tr in next 4ch sp, 3ch) twice; repeat from ★ close with sl st.

27th rnd: sl st into 4ch sp, ★ 4dbl tr cl 4ch 4dbl tr cl in 4ch sp, 1dbl tr 3ch 1dbl tr in next dbl tr, 1dbl tr in next dbl tr, 3ch, 2dbl tr cl, 4dbl tr, 2dbl tr cl, (2ch, 5dbl tr) twice, 2ch, 2dbl tr cl, 4dbl tr, 2dbl tr cl, 3ch, 1dbl tr 3ch 1dbl tr in next dbl tr, (4dbl tr cl 4ch 4dbl tr cl in next 4ch sp, 3ch, 1dbl tr in same place as last cl, in next 4ch sp work [4dbl tr cl 4ch] twice and 4dbl tr cl, 1dbl tr in next 4ch sp, 3ch) twice; repeat from ★ close with sl st.

28th rnd: sl st into 4ch sp, ★ 4dbl tr cl 4ch 4dbl tr cl in 4ch sp, 1dbl tr 3ch 1dbl tr in next dbl tr, 1dbl tr in next dbl tr, 6dbl tr cl, 3ch, 2dbl tr cl, 3dbl tr, skip 2ch, 3dbl tr, 2dbl tr cl, 3ch, 6dbl tr cl, 3ch, 1dbl tr in same place as 6dbl tr cl, 1dbl tr 3ch 1dbl tr in next dbl tr, (4dbl tr cl 4ch 4dbl tr cl in 4ch sp, 3ch, 1dbl tr in same place as last cl, 4dbl tr cl 4ch 4dbl tr cl in each of next two 4ch sps divided by 3ch, 1dbl tr in next 4ch sp, 3ch) twice; repeat from ★ close with sl st.

29th rnd: sl st into 4ch sp, ★ 4dbl tr cl 4ch 4dbl tr cl in 4ch sp, 1dbl tr 3ch 1dbl tr in next dbl tr, 1dbl tr 3ch 1dbl tr in 6dbl tr cl, 1dbl tr in next dbl tr, 3ch, 2dbl tr cl, 4dbl tr, 2dbl tr cl, 3ch, 1dbl tr in same place as last cl, 1dbl tr 3ch 1dbl tr in 6dbl tr cl, 1dbl tr 3ch 1dbl tr in next dbl tr, (4dbl tr cl 4ch 4dbl tr cl in next 4ch sp, 3ch, 1dbl tr in same place as last cl) twice, (1dbl tr in next 4ch sp, 3ch, 4dbl tr cl 4ch 4dbl tr cl in 4ch sp) twice, 3ch, 1dbl tr in same place as last cl, 4dbl tr cl 4ch 4dbl tr cl in next 4ch sp, 3ch, 1dbl tr in same place as last cl, 1dbl tr in next 4ch sp, 3ch, 4dbl tr cl 4ch 4dbl tr cl in 4ch sp, 1dbl tr in next 4ch sp, 3ch; repeat from ★ close with sl st.

30th rnd: sl st into 4ch sp, ★ 4dbl tr cl 4ch 4dbl tr cl in 4ch sp, (1dbl tr 3ch 1dbl tr in next dbl tr) twice, 1dbl tr in dbl tr, 6dbl tr cl, 3ch, 1dbl tr in same place as 6dbl tr cl, (1dbl tr 3ch 1dbl tr in next dbl tr) twice, (4dbl tr cl 4ch 4dbl tr cl in 4ch sp, 3ch, 1dbl tr in same place as last cl) twice, 4dbl tr cl 4ch 4dbl tr cl in dbl tr, (1dbl tr in next 4ch sp, 3ch, 4dbl tr cl 4ch 4dbl tr cl in 4ch sp) twice, 3ch, 1dbl tr in same place as last cl, 4dbl tr cl 4ch 4dbl tr cl in 4ch sp, 3ch, 1dbl tr in same place as last cl, 4dbl tr cl 4ch 4dbl tr cl in dbl tr, 1dbl tr in next 4ch sp, 3ch, 4dbl tr cl 4ch 4dbl tr cl in 4ch sp, 1dbl tr in next 4ch sp; repeat from ★ close with sl st.

31st rnd: sl st into 4ch sp, ★ 4dbl tr cl 4ch 4dbl tr cl in 4ch sp, (1dbl tr 3ch 1dbl tr in next dbl tr) twice, 1dbl tr in 6dbl tr cl, (1dbl tr 3ch 1dbl tr in next dbl tr) twice, (4dbl tr cl 4ch 4dbl tr cl in 4ch sp, 3ch, 1dbl tr in same place as last cl) twice, in next 4ch sp work (4dbl tr cl 4ch) twice and 4dbl tr cl, (1dbl tr in next sp, 3ch, 4dbl tr cl 4ch 4dbl tr cl in 4ch sp) twice, (3ch, 1dbl tr in same place as last cl, 4dbl tr cl 4ch 4dbl tr cl) twice, in next 4ch sp work (4dbl tr cl 4ch) twice and 4dbl tr cl, 1dbl tr in next 4ch sp, 3ch, 4dbl tr cl 4ch 4dbl tr cl in next 4ch sp, 3ch; repeat from ★ close with sl st.

32nd rnd: sl st into 4ch sp, ★ 4dbl tr cl 4ch 4dbl tr cl in 4ch sp, 1dbl tr 3ch 1dbl tr in next dbl tr, 1dbl tr, 1dbl tr 3ch 1dbl tr in next dbl tr, (4dbl tr cl 4ch 4dbl tr cl in 4ch sp, 3ch 1dbl tr in same place as last cl) twice, in each of next two 4ch sps work 4dbl tr cl 4ch 4dbl tr cl divided by 3ch, (1dbl tr in next 4ch sp, 3ch, 4dbl tr cl 4ch 4dbl tr cl in 4ch sp) twice, 3ch, 1dbl tr in same place as last cl, 4dbl tr cl 4ch 4dbl tr cl in next 4ch sp, 3ch, 1dbl tr in same place as last cl, in each of next two sps work 4dbl tr cl 4ch 4dbl tr cl divided by 3ch, 1dbl tr in next 4ch sp, 4dbl tr cl 4ch 4dbl tr cl in 4ch sp, 1dbl tr in next 4ch sp, 3ch; repeat from ★ close with sl st.

33rd rnd: sl st into 4ch sp, 4dbl tr cl 10ch 4dbl tr cl in 4ch sp, ★ 1dbl tr in dbl tr, (4dbl tr cl 10ch 4dbl tr cl) 11 times; repeat from ★ close with sl st. Fasten off.

Garland

40 cm (16") circular coffee cloth

Materials: 2 x 20g balls DMC No 40
crochet hook No 0.75

Note: Commence each round with 3ch for first treble.

Commence with 10ch, close with sl st to form a ring.
1st rnd: 3ch (for first tr), 18tr into ring, close with sl st in 3rd of 3ch.
2nd rnd: 2tr in each tr.
3rd rnd: 1tr 2ch 1tr in each tr.
4th rnd: sl st into 2ch sp, 1tr 2ch 1tr in each 2ch sp,

5th-15th Rnds: as 4th rnd, but each rnd increase between spokes by 1ch, so ending 15th rnd with 12ch between spokes.
16th rnd: sl st into 2ch sp, ★ 1tr 5ch 1tr in 2ch sp, 11ch; repeat from ★ to end of rnd, close with sl st.
17th rnd: sl st into 4ch lp, 3ch (for first tr), 8tr in same lp, 8ch, ★ 9tr in each 5ch lp, 8ch; repeat from ★ close with sl st.
18th rnd: ★ 2tr in first tr, 7tr, 2tr in last tr, 6ch; repeat from ★ close with sl st.
19th rnd: ★ 2tr in first tr, 9tr, 2tr in last tr, 5ch; repeat from ★ close with sl st.
20th rnd: ★ 1tr in first tr, (2ch, skip 1tr, 1tr in next tr) 6 times, 4ch; repeat from ★ close with sl st.
21st rnd: 3tr in each tr to end of rnd, close with sl st.
22nd rnd: ★ 1tr 1ch 1tr in first tr, (skip 2tr, 3tr in next tr) 6 times; repeat from ★ close with sl st.
23rd rnd: sl st into 1ch sp, 1tr 2ch 1tr in same sp, 2ch, skip 4tr, 3tr in next tr, (skip 2tr, 3tr in next tr) 4 times, 2ch, skip 3tr, ★ 1tr 2ch 1tr in next sp, 2ch, skip 4tr, 3tr in next tr, (skip 2tr, 3tr in next tr) 4 times, 2ch; repeat from ★ close with sl st.
24th rnd: sl st into 2ch sp, 1tr 5ch 1tr in same sp, skip 2ch and 3tr, 3tr in next tr, (skip 2tr, 3tr in next tr) 3 times, 4ch, ★ skip 3tr and 2ch sp, 1tr 5ch 1tr in next 2ch sp, 4ch, skip 2ch and 3tr, 3tr in next tr, (skip 2tr, 3tr in next tr) 3 times, 4ch; repeat from ★ close with sl st.
25th rnd: sl st into 5ch sp, ★ 9tr, 4ch, skip 4ch and 3tr, (3tr in next 2tr, skip 2tr) 3 times, 4ch; repeat from ★ close with sl st.
26th rnd: ★ 2tr in first tr, 7tr, 2tr in 9th tr, 4ch, skip 4ch and 3tr, (3tr in next tr, skip 2tr) twice, 4ch; repeat from ★ close with sl st.
27th rnd: ★ 2tr in first tr, 9tr, 2tr in 11th tr, 4ch; repeat from ★ close with sl st.
28th rnd: ★ 1tr in first tr, (2ch, 1tr in next tr) 6 times, 5ch, 1tr in second tr of grp, 5ch; repeat from ★ close with sl st.
29th rnd: ★ 3tr in first tr, (skip 2ch, 3tr in next tr) 6 times, 11ch; repeat from ★ ending with 5ch 1tr tr for last lp.
30th rnd: 3ch (for first tr), 2ch, 1tr in same sp, 6ch, ★ (skip 2tr, 3tr in next tr) 6 times, 6ch, 1tr 2ch 1tr in sixth of 11ch lp, 6ch; repeat from ★ close with sl st.
31st rnd: sl st into 2ch sp, 1tr 2ch 1tr in same 2ch sp, 7ch, ★ (skip 3tr, 3tr in next tr) 5 times, 7ch, 1tr 2ch 1tr in 2ch sp, 7ch; repeat from ★ close with sl st.
32nd rnd: sl st into 2ch sp, 1tr 2ch 1tr in same 2ch sp, 8ch, ★ (skip 3tr, 3tr in next tr) 4 times, 8ch, 1tr 2ch 1tr in 2ch sp, 8ch; repeat from ★ close with sl st.
33rd rnd: sl st into 2ch sp, in same sp work (1tr 2ch) twice and 1tr, 10ch, ★ (skip 3tr, 3tr in next tr) 3 times, 10ch, in 2ch sp work (1tr 2ch) twice and 1tr; repeat

from ★ ending with 10ch, close with sl st.

34th rnd: sl st into 2ch sp, 8ch (for first tr and 5ch), 1tr 2ch 1tr in next sp, 9ch, ★ (skip 3tr, 3tr in next tr) twice, 9ch, 1tr 2ch 1tr in 2ch sp, 5ch, 1tr 2ch 1tr in next 2ch sp, 9ch; repeat from ★ close with sl st.

35th rnd: sl st into 5ch lp, 7tr in same 5ch lp, 2ch, 1tr 2ch 1tr in next 2ch sp, 8ch, ★ skip 3tr, 3tr in next tr, 8ch, 1tr 2ch 1tr in 2ch sp, 2ch, 7tr in 5ch lp, 2ch, 1tr 2ch 1tr in 2ch sp, 8ch; repeat from ★ close with sl st.

36th rnd: 5ch (for first tr and 2ch), (skip 1tr, 1tr in next tr, 2ch) twice, 1tr in next tr, 3ch, 1tr 2ch 1tr in 2ch sp, ★ 7ch, 1dc in second tr, 7ch, 1tr 2ch 1tr in 2ch sp, 3ch, 1tr in next tr, (2ch, skip 1tr, 1tr in next tr) 3 times, 3ch, 1tr 2ch 1tr in 2ch sp; repeat from ★ ending with 7ch, 1tr 2ch 1tr in 2ch sp, 3ch, close with sl st in 3rd of 5ch lp.

37th rnd: 3tr in same place as last sl st, ★ (1tr in 2ch sp, 3tr in next tr) 3 times, 3ch, 1tr 2ch 1tr in next 2ch sp, 6ch, 1dc in dc, 6ch, 1tr 2ch 1tr in 2ch sp, 2ch 3tr in next tr; repeat from ★ ending with 6ch, 1tr 2ch 1tr in 2ch sp, 3ch, close with sl st.

38th rnd: sl st to second tr, ★ 3tr in same tr, (skip 1tr, 3tr in next tr) 6 times, 3ch, 1tr 2ch 1tr in 2ch sp, 5ch, 1dc in dc, 5ch, 1tr 2ch 1tr in next 2ch sp, 3ch; repeat from ★ close with sl st.

39th rnd: ★ 4tr in centre of each of next seven 3tr grps, 3ch, 1tr 2ch 1tr in 2ch sp, 5ch, 1dc in dc, 5ch, 1tr 2ch 1tr in 2ch sp, 3ch; repeat from ★ close with sl st.

40th rnd: sl st to second tr, ★ 2tr in same tr, 2tr in next tr, (1ch, skip 2tr, 2tr in each of next 2tr) 6 times, 3ch, 1tr 2ch 1tr in next 2ch sp, 3ch, skip dc, 1tr 2ch 1tr in next 2ch sp, 3ch, skip 1tr; repeat from ★ close with sl st.

41st rnd: sl st to second tr, ★ 2tr in same tr, 2tr in next tr, (2ch, skip 2tr, 2tr in each of next 2tr) 6 times, 4ch, 1dc in 2nd of 3ch lp, 4ch; repeat from ★ close with sl st.

42nd rnd: sl st to second tr, ★ 2tr in same tr, 2tr in next tr, (3ch, skip 2tr, 2tr in each of next 2tr) 6 times, 4ch, 1dc in dc, 4ch; repeat from ★ close with sl st.

43rd rnd: sl st to second tr, ★ 2tr in same tr, 2tr in next tr, (4ch, skip 2tr, 2tr in each of next 2tr) 6 times, 4ch, skip dc; repeat from ★ close with sl st.

44th rnd: sl st to second tr, 3ch (for first tr) 3ch, 1dc in base of 3ch (picot made), 1tr in next tr, 3ch, 1dc in centre of 4ch lp, 4ch, ★skip 1tr, 1tr in next tr, 1p, 1tr in next tr, 3ch, 1dc in centre of 4ch lp, 3ch; repeat from ★ close with sl st.

Fasten off.

MEDALLION WORK

When I researched crochet from the nineteenth and early twentieth centuries, I noted how often medallions (motifs) were used. Medallions were made into doilies, traycloths, table centres, duchess sets (or duvall sets as they were known then), table cloths, bedspreads - the list was endless.

Medallion work is fascinating. The same motif can be used to create such a variety of items. You can just let it grow to whatever size or shape you want, which against demonstrates the versatility of crochet. I have included a collection of medallion work, both squares and circles. Very often round medallions need fillers between them, but not all. Look at the 'Wagon Wheels' table centre - the medallions are small enough to connect with one another without extra filling.

Wagon Wheels

Diamond shaped table centre, 49 cm x 31 cm (19" x 12")

Materials: 2 x 20g balls DMC No 40
crochet hook No 0.7

First medallion
Commence with 6ch, close with sl st to form a ring.
1st rnd: 3ch (for first tr), 17tr; close with sl st.
2nd rnd: 1tr, 1ch; repeat to end, close with sl st.
3rd rnd: 1tr, 1tr in each ch; repeat to end, close with sl st.
4th rnd: 1tr, 1ch; repeat to end, close with sl st.

5th rnd: sl st into 1ch sp, 3ch (for first tr), skip 1sp, 1tr in next sp, 4ch, ★ 1tr in same place as last tr, skip 1sp, 1tr in next sp finishing off both tr as one, 4ch; repeat from ★ close with sl st.

6th rnd: sl st to centre of 4ch lp, 3ch (for first tr) 1tr in centre of next lp, 5ch, ★ 1tr in same place as last tr, 1tr in centre of next lp finishing off both tr as one, 5ch; repeat from ★ close with sl st.

7th rnd: 1ch, 1n each 5ch lp work: 1dc 1htr 2tr 2ch 2tr 1htr and 1dc; close with sl st. Fasten off.

Second medallion

Work as first medallion till last rnd. Connect the two medallions as follows:

In 5ch sp work: 1dc 1htr 2tr 1ch, sl st in 2ch lp of first medallion, 1ch 2tr 1htr and 1dc. Connect in this way three points.

Continue as for first medallion, close with sl st. Fasten off.

Work as many medallions as needed, connecting each one as last one. I used 25 in the cloth illustrated, but it would be simple to make it larger or smaller (36 or 16 medallions).

Buttercup

Duchess set - large mat 38 cm x 28 cm (15" x 11"); small mat 19 cm (7½") square

Materials: 3 x 20g balls DMC No 60
crochet hook No 0.75

First motif

Commence with 8ch, close with sl st to form a ring.

1st rnd: into ring work 16dc, close with sl st.

2nd rnd: 4ch, ★ 1tr in next dc, 1ch; repeat from ★ ending with sl st in third of 4ch.

3rd rnd: 5ch, ★ 1tr in tr, 2ch; repeat from ★ ending with sl st in third of 5ch.

4th rnd: 3ch, ★ 3tr in next 2ch sp, 1tr in tr, 2ch, 1tr in next tr; repeat from ★ omitting 1tr at end of last repeat, close with sl st.

5th rnd: 3ch, ★ 1tr in tr, 2tr in next tr, 1tr in each of next 2tr, 4ch, 1tr in next tr; repeat from ★ omitting 1tr at end of last repeat, close with sl st.

6th rnd: 3ch, 1tr in same place as last sl st, ★ 1tr in each of next 4tr, 2tr in next tr, 4ch, 2tr in next tr; repeat from ★ omitting 2tr at end of last repeat, close with sl st.

7th rnd: 3ch, 3tr cluster, ★ 5ch, 4tr cl, 4ch, 3dbl tr cl in next 4ch sp, 5ch, 3dbl tr cl in same sp as last cl, 4ch, 4tr cl; repeat from ★ omitting 4tr cl at end of last repeat, close with sl st in top of first cluster.

8th rnd: sl st over next 2ch, 1dc in same sp, ★ 5ch, 4 3dbl tr clusters with 3ch between each in next 5ch sp, 5ch, 1dc in next 5ch sp; repeat from ★ omitting 1dc at end of last repeat, close with sl st in first dc.

9th rnd: 4ch, 1dbl tr in cl, ★ (5ch, leaving last lp of each on hook 1dbl tr in same place as last dbl tr 1dbl tr in 3ch sp and 1dbl tr in next cl, yoh and pull through all lps on hook), 3 times, 5ch, leaving last lp of each on hook 1dbl tr in same place as last dbl tr and 1dbl tr in next dc, yoh and pull through all lps, 2ch, leaving last lp of each on hook 1dbl tr in same dc and 1dbl tr in next cl, yoh and pull through all lps on hook; repeat from ★ omitting 2dbl tr at end of last repeat, close with sl st in first dbl tr.

10th rnd: ★ 5dc in 5ch sp, 1dc in top of cl, 5ch, 1sl st in same dc (picot made); repeat from ★ twice more, 5dc in next 5ch sp, 2dc in next 2ch sp, 1dc in same sp; repeat from first ★ close with sl st in first dc. Fasten off.

Second motif

Work the same as for first motif for 9 rnds.
10th rnd: 5dc in 5ch sp, 1dc in top of next cl, 1picot, 5dc in next 5ch sp, 1dc in top of cl, 2ch, 1dc in corresponding picot of first motif, 2ch, 1sl st in last dc in of second motif, 5dc in next 5ch sp, 1dc in top of cl, 1p, 5dc in next 5ch sp, 2dc in next 2ch sp, 1p, 5dc in next 5ch sp, 1dc in top of cl, 1p 5dc in next 5ch sp, 1dc in top of next cl, 2ch, 1dc in corresponding p of first motif, 2ch, 1sl st in last dc of second motif. Complete as for first motif (no more joinings). Make necessary number of motifs, joining each as second was joined to first.

Filling

Work the same as for first 3 rnds of first motif.
4th rnd: 3ch, leaving last lp of each on hook 2tr in next sp and 1tr in next tr, yoh and pull through all lps, 6ch, 1dc in first free picot of motif, ★ 6ch, leaving last lp of each on hook 1tr in next 2tr in sp and 1tr in next tr, yoh and pull through all lps, 6ch, 1dc in next p of motif, 6ch, leaving last lp of each on hook 1tr in next tr 2tr in sp and 1tr in next tr, yoh and pull through all lps on hook, 6ch, 1dc in first free p of next motif; repeat from ★ closing with 6ch, leaving last lp of each on hook 1tr in next tr 2tr in sp and 1tr in next tr, yoh and pull through all lps on hook, 6ch, 1dc in next p of motif, 6ch, 1sl st in top of first cl.
Fasten off.
Fill in all spaces between motifs the same way.

You will need 12 motifs and 6 fillers for the large mat and 4 motifs and 1 filler for each small mat.

Pineapple

Table cloth, 88 cm (35") square

Materials: 8 x 20g balls DMC No 20
crochet hook No 1.25

First motif
Commence with 8ch, close with sl st to form a ring.
1st rnd: 16dc in ring, close with sl st.
2nd rnd: 11ch, ★ skip 3dc, 1tr 7ch 1tr in next dc, 7ch; repeat from ★ twice, 1tr in base of 11ch, 3ch, close with 1tr in 4th of 11ch.
3rd rnd: (10ch, 1dbl tr in 4th of next 7ch lp, 10ch, 1dc in next lp) 4 times, close with sl st in last tr of previous rnd.
4th rnd: sl st over 3ch, 3ch, 6tr in same lp, ★ 7ch, 7tr in next lp, 3ch, 7tr in following lp; repeat from ★ close with sl st.
5th rnd: 4ch, 1tr in tr, (1ch, 1tr) 5 times, ★ 3ch, 1dc in centre of 7ch lp, 3ch, 1tr, (1ch, 1tr) 6 times, (1ch, 1tr) 7 times; repeat from ★ close with sl st.
6th rnd: sl st over 2ch, 1dc in same sp, ★ (4ch, 1dc in next sp) 5 times, 3dc in next sp, 1dc in dc, 3dc in sp, 1dc in next sp, (4ch, 1dc in sp) 5 times, 1dc between pineapples, 1dc in next sp; repeat from ★ close with sl st.
7th rnd: sl st over 2ch, 1dc in same sp, ★ (4ch, 1dc in next sp) 4 times, 6ch, skip 3dc, 1tr in dc, 6ch, 1dc in next sp, (4ch, 1dc) 4 times, 3ch, 1dc in first lp of next pineapple; repeat from ★ close with sl st.
8th rnd: sl st over 2ch, 1dc in same sp, ★ (4ch, 1dc) 3 times, 7ch, in 1tr between next two lps work 1tr 5ch 1tr, 7ch, 1dc in next 4ch lp, (4ch, 1dc) 3 times, 5ch, 1dc in pineapple; repeat from ★ close with sl st.
9th rnd: sl st over 2ch, 1dc in same sp, ★ (4ch, 1dc in next sp) twice, 8ch, 1tr in corner tr, 5ch, 1tr in same tr, 7ch, 1tr 5ch 1tr in next tr, 8ch, 1dc in sp; repeat from ★ close with sl st.
10th rnd: sl st over 2ch, 1dc in same sp, ★ 4ch, 1dc in next sp, 11ch, 1dc in 5ch sp, 5ch, 1tr in centre of lp, 7ch, 1tr in same sp, 5ch, 1dc in 5ch lp, 11ch, 1dc in next sp; repeat from ★ close with sl st.
11th rnd: sl st over 2ch, 1dc in same sp, ★ 16ch, 1dc in 5ch lp, 10ch, 1dc in 7ch lp, ★★ 10ch, 1dc in next 5ch lp, (16ch, 1dc in next pineapple) twice; repeat from ★ close with sl st.
Fasten off.

Second motif
Repeat to ★★ in rnd 11; 5ch, sl st in first 10ch lp on one side of first motif, 5ch, 1dc in next lp of second motif, (8ch, sl st in next lp of first motif, 8ch, 1dc in next pineapple of second motif) twice, 8ch, sl st in

Above: Simplicity table cloth (page 21)

Below: Garland coffee cloth (page 32)

This page: Pineapple table cloth (page 36) and Trellis tray cloth (page 41)
Opposite: Main picture and top, Buttercup duchess set (page 40), below, Wagon Wheels tray cloth (page 34)

Above: Berkeley Square table cloth border in fillet crochet (page 46)

Left: Bread tray doily in fillet crochet (page 47)

40

next lp of first motif, 8ch, 1dc in 5ch lp of second motif, 5ch, 1sl st in next lp in first motif, 5ch, 1dc in centre of corner lp of second motif. Complete rnd as for first motif. When joining motifs on two sides repeat from **.
Make 36 motifs, joining each one as first and second motifs.

Edge
With front of work facing, attach thread to first 10ch lp on one side.
1st rnd: ★ (16ch, 1dc in centre of next 10ch lp) 3 times, (16ch, 1dc in 10ch lp) twice; repeat from ★ to corner, 16ch, 1dc in 10ch lp on next side; repeat from ★ close with sl st.
2nd rnd: 1ch, 1dc in next lp, ★ (4ch, 1dc in same lp) 6 times, 1ch, 1dc in next lp; repeat from ★ close with sl st.
3rd rnd: sl st over 2ch, 1dc in 4ch lp, ★ (4ch, 1dc in next lp) 5 times, 1dc in first lp of next scallop; repeat from ★ close with sl st.
4th rnd: sl st over dc, 1dc in 4ch lp, ★ 2ch, 1dc in next lp, 2ch, 1tr in next lp, 2ch, in same (centre) lp work (1dbl tr, 2ch) twice 1tr, (2ch, 1dc in next 4ch lp) twice, 1dc in first lp of next scallop; repeat from ★ close with sl st.
5th rnd: 1ch, 1dc in 2ch lp, ★ (4ch, 1dc in base of stitch (picot made), 1dc in next sp) 3 times, 1p in same sp, (1picot) 3 times, 1dc in first lp on next scallop; repeat from ★ close with sl st.
Fasten off.

Trellis

Traycloth, 37 cm x 29 cm (14½" x 11½")

Materials: 2 x 20g balls DMC No 20
              crochet hook No 1.00

Commence with 26ch.
1st rnd: 1tr in 8th ch from hook, ★ 2ch, skip 2ch, 1tr in next ch; repeat from ★ to end of row (7 spaces), 5ch, turn.
2nd rnd: 1tr in 2nd tr, ★ 2ch, 1tr in next tr; repeat from ★, 5ch, turn.
Repeat second row till 7 rows are completed, 1ch, do not turn, sl st to end of motif along side, 1dc.

Work now around motif as follows:
1st rnd: 6ch, skip 1sp, 4tr in next sp, 2ch, skip 1sp, 4tr in next sp, 2 ch, 10 dbl tr in corner sp, 2 ch; repeat from ★ 3 more times, skip last 2ch of last repeat and work 9dbl tr, sl st in 4th of first 8ch.

2nd rnd: 8ch, ★ 4tr in centre of sp, 4ch, work in each dbl tr: 1dbl tr 1ch, 4ch; repeat from ★ 3 more times, ending with 1ch, sl st in 4th of 8ch.
3rd rnd: sl st to centre of 4ch sp, ★ 1dc in same sp, 4ch, 1dc in centre of 4tr, 4ch, 1dc in sp, ★★ 4ch, skip first 2dbl tr, 1dc between dbl tr; repeat from ★★ 3 more times, 4ch; repeat from ★ 3 more times, 1sl st in first dc.
Fasten off.

Work second motif as first one till last rnd. Connect motifs by working each corner as follows:
(2dc, 1sl st in 4ch sp of first motif, 1dc in next sp of second motif) twice.

Make and connect as many motifs as are needed. Traycloth has 20 motifs in 4 rows of 5.

Edge
1st rnd: in each sp work 1dc, 4ch; close with sl st.
2nd rnd: ★ 1dc in sp, in next sp work (2dbl tr puff st, 3ch) twice 2dbl tr puff st, 1dc in next sp; repeat from ★ to corner lps which are worked as follows: 1dc in sp, (2dbl tr puff st, 3ch) 3 times, 2dbl tr puff st, repeat from ★ close with sl st.
Fasten off.

Trellis

Sandwich tray doily, 23 cm x 12 cm (9" x 4¾")

Materials: 1 x 20g ball DMC No 60
                    crochet hook No 0.75

This small sandwich doily is worked in the same way as the traycloth, but with 2 rows of 4 motifs, using a finer cotton.

Periwinkle

Sandwich tray doily, 31 cm x 14 cm (12" x 5½")

Materials: 1 x 20g ball DMC No 40
                    crochet hook No 0.75

First Medallion
Commence with 6ch, close with sl st to form a ring.
1st rnd: 4ch (for first dbl tr) ★ 3dbl tr cl, 4ch, 1dbl tr, 4ch; repeat from ★ 5 more times (6 clusters made), close with sl st.
2nd rnd: in every sp work 1dc 3tr 1dc; close with sl st.
3rd rnd: 9ch, ★ 1tr between two dc, 6ch; repeat from ★ close with sl st in 3rd of 9ch.
4th rnd: in every sp work 1dc 1tr 2dbl tr 1tr and 1dc; close with sl st.
5th rnd: 7ch, 1tr in same sp, 4ch, ★ 1tr, 4ch, 1tr between cls, 4ch; repeat from ★ close with sl st in 3rd of 7ch.
6th rnd: sl st into V-sp and work in same sp:
3dbl tr cl 4ch 1dbl tr 4ch 3dbl tr cl, 4ch, 4dc in next V-sp, 4ch; repeat from ★ close with sl st in top of first cluster.
7th rnd: sl st into sp, in every sp work 1dc 1tr 2dbl tr 1tr and 1dc, 3ch, 1dc in centre dc, 3ch; repeat from ★ close with sl st.
Fasten off.

Work 2 more medallions and join 2 points with 1dc 1tr 1dbl tr 1ch, sl st between 2dbl tr of previous medallion.
Finish with lace edge around the medallions:
1st rnd: in centre of each grp of tr work 1tr 4ch and 1tr, 2ch, (leave out 2ch between medallions where they are joined).

2nd rnd: ★ 4ch, ★★ 1tr in second tr, 6ch, 1tr in next tr; repeat from ★★ till sp between medallions is reached and then work into st between V-sp of previous row 2ch 1tr 4ch 1tr and 2ch; repeat from ★ to end of rnd, close with sl st.

3rd rnd: 8ch, 1tr in same sp, 4ch, ★ 1tr 4ch 1tr in st between next 2tr, 4ch; repeat till end of rnd leaving out 4ch between V-sp where the medallions are joined, close with sl st in 3rd of 8ch.

4th rnd: sl st into sp, 3tr in same sp, 1tr in tr; repeat from ★ to end of rnd, close with sl st.

5th rnd: 6ch, skip 1tr, ★ 1tr in next tr, 2ch, skip 1tr; repeat from ★ to end of rnd leaving out 2ch twice where medallions meet, close with sl st.

6th rnd: sl st into sp, ★ 1dc, 4ch, skip 1sp, into next sp work (3dbl tr cl 3ch 1dbl tr 3ch 3dbl tr cl and 3ch) twice, 3dbl tr cl, 4ch, skip 1sp, 1dc in each of next 8 spaces; repeat from ★ close with sl st.

7th rnd: sl st into sp, ★ in every sp work 1dc 3tr 1dc, e3dc, 4ch, skip 2dc, 3dc; repeat from ★ close with sl st.

8th rnd: 7ch, ★★ 1tr in dc between cl, 4ch; repeat from ★★ 6 more times, 3ch, 1dc in sp, 3ch, 1tr in dc before cl; repeat from ★★ to end of rnd, close with sl st in 3rd of 7ch.

9th rnd: sl st into sp, in same sp work ★★ 1dc 3tr 1dc; repeat from ★★ in each of next 5 spaces, 1dc in next sp; repeat from ★★ to end of rnd, close with sl st. Fasten off.

FILLET CROCHET

Fillet crochet is one of the oldest forms of crochet. It is simple to do, and uses only two main stitches: a treble and a chain stitch. Worked in fine cotton with a small crochet hook, it resembles fine filigree lace, and is ideal for decorating bed linen, towels and lingerie and for making curtains and bedspreads.

Fillet crochet consists of blocks and spaces and often incorporates lacets, like 'Berkeley Square', the tablecloth with crochet edge on page 46, and some of the shelf edgings. Lacets are an attractive way of filling in large areas.

The charts which are often used with fillet crochet are easy to follow. You work the uneven rows from right to left and the even rows from left to right.

Counted cross stitch charts can make good charts for fillet crochet. The 'Peony' cushion on page 53 has been worked from a counted cross stitch chart, as has the 'Mosaic' insertion on page 81.

Always begin your fillet crochet with 3 chain stitches for the first treble, and work your last stitch in the turning chain.

A filled block (or square) has 4 trebles and a space is 2 chain stitches, skipping 2 stitches from the previous row. The last treble of a block is also the first treble of the following block, that is, 2 blocks next to one another consist of 7 trebles.

Sounds complicated? Not really. Try one of the patterns, and you will find out how easy it is.

Fillet crochet needs careful pinning out. Moisten lace and pin out on a towel to the correct measurements, then leave to dry.

Special terms

Block (or square) = 4 trebles
Space = 2 chain, skip 2 stitches, 1 treble

Lacets consist of one row of bars and one row of lacets:
Bar = 1 treble, 5 chain, skip 5 stitches, 1 treble
Lacet = 1 treble, 3 chain, 1 double crochet in centre of 5 chain loop, 3 chain, 1 treble

When I made my first piece of fillet crochet many years ago, I was disappointed as the squares were not square enough for my liking. Over the years I have developed a treble stitch which is slightly longer than an ordinary treble stitch, but not as long as a double treble (which is too long). I use this treble for all my fillet crochet. Have a look at the following drawings. This stitch has one more movement in the treble, and is quite easy to master.

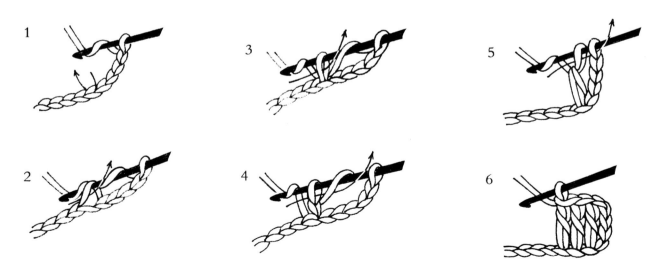

Roses

Table runner, 80 cm x 36 cm (32" x 14")

Materials:　5 x 20g balls DMC No 20
　　　　　　crochet hook No 1.00

Commence with 178ch (175 + 3).
1st row: 1tr in 4th ch from hook, 174tr, 3ch, turn.
2nd row: 3tr, 3ch, skip 2tr, 1dc in next tr, 3ch, skip 2tr,
★ 1tr in next tr, 3ch, skip 2tr, 1dc in next tr, 3ch, skip
2tr; repeat from ★ to last 4tr, 4tr, 3ch, turn.
3rd row: 3tr, 5ch, ★ 1tr, 5ch; repeat from ★ to last 4tr,
4tr, 3ch, turn.
4th row: 3tr, 3ch, 1dc in 3rd ch of 5ch lp, 3ch, ★ 1tr in
tr, 3ch, 1dc in third of 5ch lp, 3ch; repeat from ★ to
last 4tr, 4tr, 3ch, turn.
Repeat 3rd and 4th rows once, then 3rd row once
more.
8th row: 3tr, 3ch, 1dc in 3rd of 5ch lp, 3ch, (1tr, 3ch,
1dc in 3rd of 5ch lp, 3ch) twice (3 lacets made), (1tr
in tr, 5tr in 5ch lp) 21 times, 3 lacets, 4tr, 3ch, turn.
9th row: 3tr, 3 lacets, 4tr, (2ch, skip 2tr, 1tr in next tr)
42 times (42 spaces), 4tr, 3 lacets, 4tr, 3ch, turn.
Work another 2 rows with 42 spaces.
Work following chart for roses, beginning with
17 spaces, and continuing the lacets edge.
Finish with spaces and lacets rows to correspond with
beginning.
Do not cut thread.

Border
1st rnd: 3ch (for first tr), 5ch, 1tr in same place as 3ch,
★ 2ch, 1tr in beginning of row; repeat from ★ all
around runner, working 1tr 5ch 1tr in each corner.
2nd rnd: ★ in corner work 4tr 5ch 4tr, (2sps, 4tr)
17 times, 2sps, (4tr, 3sps) 18 times, 4tr 5ch 4tr in
corner, (3sps, 4tr) 7 times, 2sps, (4tr, 3sps) 7 times;
repeat from ★ to end of rnd, close with sl st.
3rd rnd: ★ 4tr 5ch 4tr in corner, (1 sp, 4tr) 36 times,
4sps, (4tr, 1sp) 33 times, 3sps, in corner, (1 sp, 4tr)

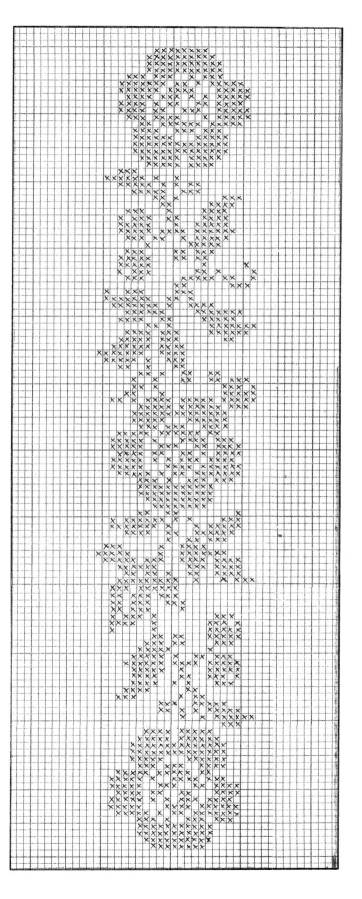

14 times, 4sps, (4tr, 1sp) 14 times; repeat from ★ to end of rnd, close with sl st.

4th rnd: ★ 4tr 5ch 4tr in corner, (3sps, 4tr) 17 times, 6sps, (4tr, 3sps) 18 times, 4tr 5ch 4tr in corner, (3sps, 4tr) 7 times, 6sps, (4tr, 3sps) 7 times; repeat from ★ to end of rnd, close with sl st.

5th rnd: ★ 1tr 2ch spaces all around runner, in each corner work 1tr 5ch 1tr in third of 5ch lp, 2ch.

6th rnd: 3ch (for first tr), 4tr in same place, 1dc in next tr, ★ 5tr in next tr, 1dc in next tr; repeat from ★; in each corner work 5tr, 1dc in centre of 5ch lp, 5tr. Fasten off.

Berkeley Square
Table cloth with crochet border, 72 cm (28") square

Materials: 4 x 20g balls DMC No 20
1 ball DMC No 40
43 cm (17") linen square
crochet hooks Nos 1.00 and 0.75

Using crochet hook No 1.00 and DMC No 20 commence with 67ch.

1st row: 1tr in 4th ch from hook, 5tr, 2 lacets, 4tr, 2ch, skip 2ch, 1tr, 3ch, skip 2ch, 1dc, 3ch, skip 2ch, 1tr, 2ch, skip 2ch, 4tr, 4 lacets, 4tr, 3ch, turn.

2nd row: 3tr, 4 bars of 5ch, 7tr, 5ch, 7tr, 2 bars, 7tr, 9ch, turn.

3rd row: 1tr in 4th ch from hook, 5tr, 3 lacets, 19tr, 4 lacets, 4tr, 3ch, turn.

4th row: 3tr, 4 bars, 19tr, 3 bars, 7tr, 9ch, turn.

5th row: 1tr in 4th ch from hook, 5tr, 2 lacets, 13tr, 6sps, 1tr, 13tr, 2 lacets, 4tr, 3ch, turn.

6th row: 3tr, 2 bars of 5ch, 1sp, 10tr, 6sps, 10tr, 1sp, 2 bars, 7tr, 9ch, turn.

7th row: 1tr in 4th tr from hook, 5tr, 4 lacets, 7tr, 6sps, 7tr, 3 lacets, 4tr, 3ch, turn.

8th row: 3tr, 3 bars, 7tr, 6sps, 7tr, 4 bars, 7tr, turn.

9th row: sl st over 7tr, 3ch (for first tr), 6tr, 2 lacets, 1sp, 10tr, 6sps, 10tr, 1sp, 2 lacets, 4tr, 3ch, turn.

10th row: 3tr, 2 bars, 13tr, 6sps, 13tr, 2 bars, 7tr, turn.

11th row: sl st over block, 3ch, 6tr, 3 lacets, 19tr, 4 lacets, 4tr, 3ch, turn.

12th row: 3tr, 4 bars, 19tr, 3 bars, 7tr, turn.

13th row: sl st over block, 3ch, 6tr, 2 lacets, 7tr, 1 lacet, 7tr, 4 lacets, 4tr, 3ch, turn.

14th row: 3tr, 4 bars, 4tr, 1sp, 5ch, 1tr, 2ch, 4tr, 2 bars, 7tr, turn.

15th row: sl st over block, 3ch, 6tr, 8 lacets, 4tr, 3ch, turn.

16th row: 3tr, 8 bars, 7tr, turn.

Commence corner:

17th row: sl st over block, 3ch, 6tr, 7 lacets, 8ch, turn.

18th row: 1tr in 2nd tr from hook, 6 more bars, 7tr, 9ch, turn.

19th row: 1tr in 4th ch from hook, 5tr, 8 lacets, 8ch, turn.

20th row: 8 bars, 7tr, 9ch, turn.

21st row: 1tr in 4th ch from hook, 5tr, 2 lacets, 4tr, 1sp, 1 lacet, 1sp, 4tr, 4 lacets, 8ch, turn.

22nd row: 4 bars, 7tr, 5ch, 7tr, 2 bars, 7tr, 9ch, turn.

23rd row: 1tr in 4th ch from hook, 5tr, 3 lacets, 19tr, 4 lacets, 8ch, turn.

24th row: 4 bars, 19tr, 3 bars, 7tr, 9ch, turn.

25th row: 1tr in 4th ch from hook, 5tr, 2 lacets, 13tr, 6sps, 13tr, 2 lacets, 8ch, turn.

26th row: 2 bars, 1sp, 10tr, 6sps, 10tr, 1sp, 2 bars, 7tr, 9ch, turn.

27th row: 1tr in 4th ch from hook, 5tr, 4 lacets, 7tr, 6sps, 3 lacets, 8ch, turn.

28th row: 3 bars, 7tr, 6sps, 7tr, 4 bars, 7tr, turn.

29th row: sl st over block, 3ch (for first tr), 6tr, 2 lacets, 1sp, 10tr, 6sps, 10tr, 1sp, 2 lacets, 8ch, turn.

30th row: 2 bars, 13tr, 6sps, 13tr, 2 bars, 7tr, turn.

31st row: sl st over block, 3ch (for 1tr), 6tr, 3 lacets, 19tr, 3 lacets, 7tr, 3ch, turn.

32nd row: 6tr, 3 bars, 19tr, 3 bars, 7tr, turn.

33rd row: sl st over block, 3ch, 6tr, 2 lacets, 7tr, 1 lacet, 7tr, 2 lacets, 7tr, 3ch, turn.

34th row: 6tr, 2 bars, 4tr, 1sp, 1 bar, 1sp, 4tr, 2 bars, 7tr, turn.

35th row: sl st over block, 3ch, 6tr, 5 lacets, 7tr, 3ch, turn.

36th row: 6tr, 5 bars, 7tr, turn.

37th row: sl st over block, 3ch, 6tr, 3 lacets, 7tr, 3ch, turn.

38th row: 6tr, 3 bars, 7tr, turn.

39th row: sl st over block, 3ch, 6tr, 1 lacet, 7tr, 3ch, turn.

40th row: 6tr, 5ch, 7tr, turn.

41st row: sl st over block, 3ch, 6tr, 3ch, turn and work 6tr in top of 6tr, break off yarn.

Join yarn at end of 32nd row, 9ch, turn.

42nd row: 1tr in 4th chain from hook, 5tr, 8 lacets, slip in top of tr in 17th row, sl st over next block, 3ch, turn.

43rd row: 3tr, 8 bars, 7tr, 9ch, turn.

44th row: 1tr in 4th ch from hook, 5tr, 2 lacets, 4tr, 1sp, 1 lacet, 1sp, 4tr, 4 lacets, 4tr, 3ch, turn.

Continue from 2nd row of pattern for length required.

Fasten off.

Make a narrow hem around piece of linen, and crochet around it with DMC No 40 and crochet hook No 0.75, working around linen in 1dc, 1ch; ease around corners to keep them square.

Close crochet border with small over-and-over stitches.

To mount crochet to linen oversew crochet border onto dc with small stitches.

Bread Tray Doily

Rectangular doily, 29 cm x 17 cm (11½" x 6½")

Materials: 1 x 20g ball DMC No 20
crochet hook No 1.25

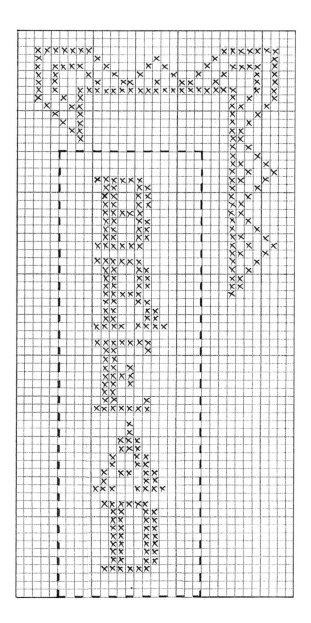

Commence with 56ch (51 + 5).

1st row: 1tr in 8th ch from hook, ★ 2ch, skip 2ch, 1tr in next ch; repeat from ★ (17sps), 5ch, turn.

2nd row: ★ skip 2ch, 1tr in next tr; repeat from ★ 5ch, turn.

Work according to chart, ending with 2 rows of 17sps.

Edge

Begin at a corner and attach thread, 3ch, 2tr in side of tr, 1tr in ch row, 2tr in each sp, 1tr in tr.

Work like this to the next corner, 3ch, 2tr in side of turning tr, 1tr in ch row; continue as before to end of rnd, close with sl st.

Follow chart for border and fasten off.

Classic

Doily, 23 cm (9") square

Materials: 1 x 20g ball DMC No 40
               crochet hook No 0.75

Commence with 141ch (136 + 5).
1st row: 1tr in 8th ch from hook, ★ 2ch, skip 2ch, 1tr in next tr; repeat from ★ (45sps).
Work according to chart, beginning and ending each row with 1 space.

Edge
Work around doily as follows:
1st rnd: 2tr in each sp, 1tr in tr; in corners work 2tr 4ch 2tr, close with sl st.
2nd rnd: ★ 1tr 1picot 1tr in tr, skip 2tr, work from ★ to corner, 1tr 1p 1tr in 4ch lp; repeat from ★ to end of row, close with sl st.
Fasten off.

Roses table runner in fillet crochet (page 45)

Classic doily in fillet crochet (page 48)

49

Cushions clockwise from top: Sunbeam (page 55), Peony (page 53), Cockle Shells (page 54) and Classic (page 53), with detail of Classic at left.

*Handkerchief edgings, clockwise from top left
Mary-Bridget, Maryanne, Klasina and Norah (pages
56-57)*

Rainbow bathtowel edging (page 59)

From top to bottom: Petal face washer edging (page 66), Kathy handtowel edging (page 65) and Wrought Iron bathtowel edging (page 58)
Below: Petite face washer edging (page 66), Sheena handtowel edging (page 60) and Lotus bathtowel edging (page 58)

CUSHIONS

Clockwise from top left: Classic, Cockle Shells, Peony and Sunbeam

Classic

Square cushion, 33cm (13")

Materials: 1 ball DMC 'Maéva' (approx equal to No 10 cotton)
crochet hook No 1.50

Use pattern from doily 'Classic' on page 48, omitting border.

Commence with 132ch (129 + 3).
1st row: 1tr in 4th ch from hook, 1tr in each ch (129tr and turning ch) 3ch, turn.
2nd row: 3tr, 41 spaces, 4tr, 3ch, turn.
Follow chart from page 48.

Peony

Square cushion, 35 cm (13¾")

This design shows the versatility of fillet crochet. It has been worked from a counted cross stitch pattern.

Materials: 2 x 20g balls DMC No10
crochet hook No 1.75

Commence with 210ch (207 + 3).
1st row: 3ch (for first tr), 206tr, 3ch, turn.
Work according to the chart on the next page, beginning and ending each row with 4tr.

Stitch chart for Peony cushion on previous page

Cockle Shells

Square cushion, 30 cm (12")

Materials: 2 x 20g balls DMC No 20
crochet hook No 1.25

First motif

Commence with 8ch, close with sl st to form a ring.

1st rnd: 3ch (for first tr), 3tr, (4ch, 4tr) 3 times, 4ch, close with sl st in third of 3ch.

2nd rnd: ★ 1tr in each tr, in sp work 3tr 4ch 3tr (corner); repeat from ★ close with sl st.

3rd, 4th and 5th rnds: as 2nd rnd.

6th rnd: 3ch, 1tr in each of next 3tr, 4ch, skip 4tr, 1tr in each of next 4tr, ★ 4ch, 1n corner sp work 3tr 4ch 3tr, (4ch, skip 4tr, 1tr in each of next 4tr) 3 times; repeat from ★ ending with 4ch, sl st in 3rd of 3ch.

7th rnd: sl st over next 3tr and into sp, 3ch, 3tr in same sp, 4ch, skip 4tr, 4tr in next sp, ★ 4ch, in corner sp work 3tr 4ch 3tr, (4ch, 4tr in next sp) 4 times; repeat from ★ ending as before.

8th rnd: sl st over next 3tr and into sp, 3ch, 3tr in same sp, 4ch, 4tr in next sp, ★ 4ch, in corner sp work 3tr 4ch 3tr, (4ch, 4tr in next sp) 5 times; repeat from ★ ending as before.

54

9th rnd: 3ch, 1tr in each of next 3tr, 4ch, 1dc in each of next 4tr, ★ 4ch, in corner sp work 12tr, (4ch, skip 1sp, 1dc in each of next 4tr, 4ch, skip 1sp, 1tr in each of next 4tr) twice, 1dc in each of next 4tr; repeat from ★ ending as before.

10th and 11th rnds: 3ch, 1tr in each of next 3tr, 1dc in each dc, ★ 4ch, (1tr in next tr, 1ch) 11 times, 1tr in next tr, (4ch, 1dc in each of next 4dc, 4ch, 1tr in each of next 4tr) twice, 4ch, 1dc in each of next 4dc; repeat from ★ ending as before.

12th rnd: 3ch, 1tr in each of next 3tr, 4ch, 1dc in each of next 4dc, ★★ 4ch, 1dc in next tr, ★ 4ch, 1dc in 4th ch from hook (picot made), 1dc in next sp; repeat from ★ 10 times, 1p in next tr, (12 picots made), (4ch, 1dc in each of next 4dc, 4ch, 1tr in each of next 4tr) twice, 4ch, 1dc in each of next 4dc; repeat from ★★ all round, ending as before.
Fasten off.

Second motif

Work as first motif to 12th rnd.
12th rnd: work as for first motif until 8th picot is completed, 1dc in next sp, 1dc in next tr, 2ch, sl st in corresponding picot of first motif, 2ch, 1dc in 2nd ch from joining (thus joining corresponding picots), 1dc in next sp; continue rnd as for first motif, joining 3 picots and first 4 picots of next corner to corresponding picots of first motif.

Sew corresponding tr scallops with neat over-and-over stitches.

Make 2 more motifs, joining them as second motif was joined to first, leaving centre picots of each corner free.

Sunbeam

Round cushion, 35 cm (13¾")

Materials: 1 ball DMC 'Maéva' (approx. equal to No 10 cotton)
crochet hook No 1.75

Commence with 6ch, close with sl st to form a ring.
1st rnd: 4ch, 1tr, ★ (1ch, 1tr) 9 times, close with sl st in 3rd of 4ch (10 spaces made).
2nd rnd: sl st into first sp, 1dc in same sp, (2ch, 1dc in next sp) 9 times, close with sl st.
3rd rnd: sl st into 2ch sp, 4ch, 1tr in same sp, 2ch, 1tr 1ch 1tr in next sp, 2ch) 9 times; close with sl st inn 3rd of 4ch.

4th rnd: 1tr 1ch 1tr in every 1ch sp separated by 3ch; close with sl st.
5th rnd: as 4th rnd, but with 6ch between.
6th rnd: as 4th rnd, but with 7ch between.
7th rnd: as 4th rnd, but with 8ch between.
8th rnd: as 4th rnd, but with 10ch between.
9th rnd: as 4th rnd, but with 11ch between.
10th rnd: as 4th rnd, but with 13ch between.
11th rnd: sl st into sp, 1tr 1ch 1tr in same sp, ★ 7ch, 1dc in 7th ch of 13ch lp, 7ch, 1tr 1ch 1tr in next sp; repeat from ★ close with sl st.
12th rnd: sl st into sp, 4ch, 1tr in same sp, ★ 7ch, 1tr 1ch 1tr in dc, 7ch, 1tr 1ch 1tr in next sp; repeat from ★ close with sl st in 3rd of 4ch (20 grps made).
13th-20th rnds: as 4th rnd, each ch lp to increase by 1ch, thus working 15ch in 20th rnd.
21st rnd: As 20th rnd, but with 2ch between trs. Close with sl st.
22nd rnd: sl st into 2ch sp, 5ch (for first tr tr), 9tr tr in same sp, ★ 10ch, 10tr tr in next 2ch sp; repeat from ★ close with sl st.
23rd rnd: 1dc in first tr tr, 12ch, 1dc in last tr tr, ★ 5ch, 1dc in centre of 10ch lp, 5ch, 1dc in first tr tr, 12ch, 1dc in last tr tr; repeat from ★ close with sl st in 5th of 5ch.
24th rnd: ★ 6dc, 4ch, 1dc in base of 4ch (picot made), 6dc, 5ch, 1dc in dc, 5ch; repeat from ★ close with sl st.
Fasten off.

HANDKERCHIEF EDGINGS

Clockwise from top left: Mary-Bridget, Maryanne, Klasina and Norah

Materials: handkerchiefs
DMC No 60
crochet hook No 0.75

One 20 g ball of DMC No 60 makes approximately 4
handkerchief edges.

3rd rnd: sl st into first 4ch lp, 3ch (for first tr), in
each lp work: 3tr 3ch 3tr, 1dc in next lp. In corner lp
work 4tr 3ch 4tr; close with sl st in 3rd of 3ch lp.
4th rnd: ★ 1dc in each tr, 4ch, 1dc in base st (picot
made), in corners work: 3dc, skip 1tr, 3p, skip 1tr,
3dc; repeat from ★ to end of rnd, close with sl st.
Fasten off.

Norah

Commence 9 holes before corner.
1st rnd: dc around 4 sides, 3dc in each corner, close
with sl st in first dc.
2nd rnd: ★ (4ch, skip 3dc, 1dc) twice, 4ch around
corner, 1dc; work this way around handkerchief (41
4ch lps on each side, or an uneven number), and one
4ch lp on each corner.

Klasina

Commence 7 holes from corner.
1st rnd: 1dc in every hole, work 3dc in each corner,
close with sl st.
2nd rnd: 5dc, 5ch round corner, ★ 5dc, 5ch, skip 4dc;
repeat from ★ to end of rnd, taking care to have a
5ch lp on each corner.

3rd rnd: in each 5ch lp work: (3dbl tr cl, 3ch) 3 times, 3dbl tr cl, 1dc in 3rd of 5dc of previous rnd. In each corner work: (3dbl tr cl, 3ch) 4 times, 3dbl tr cl, close with sl st.

4th rnd: sl st to first 3ch lp of corner, in each corner work: 3tr in first lp, 4dbl tr in each of next 2lps, 3tr in last lp, ★ skip 1dc, 3tr 4dbl tr 3tr in next three 3ch lps; repeat from ★ to end of rnd, working each corner as first corner, close with sl st in first tr of corner.

5th rnd: sl st to first tr, in each corner work: 3dc, (1tr, 3dbl tr, 1tr, 1dc between 4tr grps) twice, 3dc, ★ 1tr, 2dbl tr, 1tr, 6dc; repeat from ★ to end of rnd, taking care to work each corner as first corner, close with sl st.

Fasten off.

Mary-Bridget

Commence 10 holes before corner.

1st rnd: 1dc in each hole, in corners, work (1dc, 1ch) twice, 1dc; close with sl st.

2nd rnd: 3dc, 3ch, skip 2dc, 3dc, 5ch in corner, 3dc, ★ 3ch, 3dc; repeat from ★ working 5ch in each corner.

3rd rnd: sl st to first 3ch lp, in each 3ch lp work: 3tr 3ch 3tr, in each 5ch corner lp work: (3tr, 3ch) twice, 3tr.

4th rnd: sl st to first 3ch lp, 1dc, 1p, 1dc in same sp, in the two corner sps work: (1dbl tr, 1p) 4 times, 1dbl tr, ★ 1dc 1p 1dc in next sp, in following sp work: (1dbl tr, 1p) 5 times, 1dbl tr; repeat from ★ to end of rnd, working the corners the same as the first corner, close with sl st.

Fasten off.

Maryanne

Commence 7 holes before corner.

1st rnd: 1dc in every hole, 3dc in each corner.

2nd rnd: ★ skip 2dc, 2tr 2dbl tr 2tr in next dc, skip 2dc, 3dc; in each corner work: 2tr 3dbl tr 2tr; repeat from ★ to end of rnd, close with sl st.

3rd rnd: sl st to top of grp, ★ 1dc between 2dbl tr, 5ch, 1tr in last tr, 1tr in 2nd tr of next grp, 5ch; in each corner work: 1tr in tr, 6ch, 1dc in centre dbl tr, 6ch, 1tr in next tr; repeat from ★ to end of rnd, close with sl st.

4th rnd: in each 6ch lp work 8dc.

5th rnd: ★ 3dc, 4ch, 1dc in base of 4ch (picot made), 3dc; repeat from ★ over each bow, close with sl st.

Fasten off.

BATH TOWEL EDGINGS

All towel edgings begin with one row of 1dc, 1ch, worked evenly along towel edge.

For ease of working you may use a finer crochet hook for this first row; the smaller hook goes more easily through the towelling and won't make holes. Remember to change the hook for a larger size after this row, or your work will become too tight.

Materials: 1 bath towel
1 ball DMC 'Hermina' or equivalent 4-ply cotton
crochet hook No 2.50

Wrought Iron

1st row: 1tr, 2ch evenly spaced over dc row.
2nd row: 3ch, 1dc in first sp, (3ch, 1dc) twice, ★ 8ch, skip 1sp, 1dc, (3ch, 1dc) 7 times; repeat from ★ ending with 8ch, 1dc, (3ch, 1dc) 3 times, 1ch, turn.
3rd row: 1dc in sp, 3ch, 1dc, 2ch, skip 1sp, ★ in 8ch lp

Clockwise from the bottom: Wrought Iron bathtowel edging (this page), Petal face washer edging (page 66 and Kathy handtowel edging (page 65)

work: (1dbl tr, 2ch) 7 times, 1dbl tr, skip 1sp, 1dc, (3ch, 1dc) 4 times, 2ch; repeat from ★ ending with (1dbl tr, 2ch) 7 times, 1dbl tr, 2ch, 1dc, (3ch, 1dc) 3 times, 2ch, turn.
4th row: 2ch, ★ in each dbl tr work: 3dbl tr cl, 3ch, (8dbl tr cl made), skip 1sp, 1dc in each of next 2sps; repeat from ★ ending with 1dc in last lp, sl st to first row, 3ch, turn.
5th row: 1tr in third row, ★ 1tr in top of every dbl tr cl with 4ch between each.
Work across from one scallop to the other without ch between, end with 1tr in third row, 1tr in base row, 3ch, turn.
6th row: work 3dbl tr cl in top of every tr, with 5ch between each and work across from scallop to scallop without ch between.
7th row: 1 picot, 6dc over each 5ch lp, 1 p over every dbl tr cl, end with picot.
Fasten off.

Lotus

Note: 4ch turning ch counts as first dbl tr of next row.

Commence with 1dc, 1ch along edge of towel, 4ch, turn.
1st row: 3dbl tr in first dc, ★ 3ch, skip 3dc, 4dc, 3ch, in 4th dc work: 4dbl tr 3ch 4dbl tr; repeat from ★ to end of row, 4ch, turn.
2nd row: ★ 6dbl tr over 4dbl tr, 2ch, 1tr in centre dc, 2ch, 6dbl tr over 4dbl tr, 3ch, 1dbl tr in lp, 3ch; repeat from ★ to end of row, 4ch, turn.
3rd row: ★ 6dbl tr cl, 5ch, 6dbl tr cl, 5tr (2 either side and one in centre), 5ch; repeat from ★ to end of row, 4ch, turn.
4th row: ★ 6dbl tr, 4ch, 6dbl tr between 6dbl tr cl of previous row, 3ch, 1tr in centre tr, 3ch; repeat from ★ to end of row, 4ch, turn.
5th row: ★ 6dbl tr, 4ch, 1dbl tr in lp, 4ch, 6dbl tr, 2ch, 1dbl tr in tr, 2ch; repeat from ★ to end of row, turn.
6th row: sl st in 2nd dbl tr, 4ch, 2dbl tr cl in next 2dbl tr, 4ch, sl st in 5th dbl tr of previous row, ★ in each lp work: 3dc, 1p, 3dc, sl st in 2nd dbl tr, 4ch, 3dbl tr cl, 3dbl tr cl in next leaf, 4ch, sl st in 5th tr of leaf; repeat from ★ to end of row.
Fasten off.

Rainbow

1st row: 1ch, 1dc in every st, 1ch, turn.
2nd row: 1dc, 3ch, skip 2dc, 1dc, 3ch, 3dc, ★ 5ch, skip 3dc, 3dc, (3ch, 1dc) 3 times, 3ch, 3dc; repeat from ★ to end of row ending with two lps of 3ch, 5ch, turn.
3rd row: 1dc in first lp, 3ch, 1dc in next lp, ★ (1dbl tr, 1ch) 7 times, 1dbl tr in 5ch lp, 1dc in next lp, 3ch, 1dc, 5ch, 1dc, 3ch, 1dc; repeat from ★ to end of row ending with 3ch, 1dc, 5ch, 1dc, 1ch, turn.
4th row: sl st to centre of 5ch lp, 1dc, 2ch, (1dbl tr, 2ch) 7 times, 1dbl tr, 2ch, 1dc in centre of 5ch lp; repeat from ★ to end of row, 1dc in last dc, turn.
5th row: sl st to sp between first and second dbl tr, 1dc, ★ 7ch, turn, skip 3ch, 2tr, 2dbl tr, skip 1sp between dbl tr of previous row, 1dc, make another 2 points with 7ch (like last one), 1dc in last sp, 3ch, 1dc across to 1st sp of next scallop; repeat from ★ to end of row, sl st to base row, 3ch, turn.
6th row: (1dc, 3ch) twice, ★ 1dc in top of point, (4ch, 1dbl tr in dc between points, 4ch, 1dc in next point) twice, 3ch; repeat from ★ to end of row, ending with dc in last dbl tr and 3ch lps to base row, turn.
7th row: 1dc in first lp, (5ch, 1dc in next lp) 6 times, 3ch, 1dc in 3ch lp, 3ch, ★ (1dc in next lp, 5ch) 3 times, 1dc in next lp, 3ch, 1dc in 3ch lp, 3ch;

repeat from ★ to end of row ending with six 5ch lps, dc in base row.
8th row: 2 p in each 5ch lp, 1p in each 3ch lp. Fasten off.

Wheat

1st row: 1dc in first dc, 3ch, skip 2sts, ★ 2tr in next st, 5ch, 1sl st on base of 5ch (picot made), 1tr in next st, 3ch, skip 2sts, 1dc in next st, 3ch, skip 2sts, 1tr, 3ch, 1tr in next st, 3ch, skip 2sts, 1dc in next st, 3ch, skip 2sts; repeat from ★ ending with 1tr, 1p, 2tr, 3ch, turn.
2nd row: 1tr in tr of last row, 1p, 1tr in next tr, ★ 3ch, skip 2sps, 1tr in tr, 2tr, 2ch, 2tr in 3ch sp, 1tr in tr, 3ch, skip 2sps, 1tr in tr, 1p, 2tr; repeat from ★ ending with 3ch, turn.
3rd row: ★ 1tr in tr, 1p, 1tr in tr, 3ch, 1tr in each of next 3tr, 1tr, 2ch, 1tr in 2ch sp, 1tr in each of next 3tr, 3ch; repeat from ★ to end of row, ending with 1tr, 1p, 2tr, 3ch, turn.
4th row: ★ 1tr in tr, 1p, 1tr in tr, 4ch, skip 2tr, 1tr in each of next 2tr, 1tr, 2ch, 1tr in 2ch sp, 1tr in each of next 2tr, 4ch; repeat from ★ to end of row, ending with 1tr, 1p, 2tr, 3ch, turn.
5th row: ★ 1tr in tr, 1p, 1tr in tr, 5ch, skip 2tr, 1tr in next tr and 1tr in 2ch sp making these last 2tr into a cl, 1p, 1tr in 2ch sp and 1tr in tr making the last two tr into a cl, 5ch; repeat from ★ to end of row ending with 1tr, 1p, 2tr. Fasten off.

HANDTOWEL EDGINGS

With right side of towel facing, and beginning at right hand corner, work evenly along edge of towel; 1dc, 1ch, to next corner, 3ch, turn.

Materials: handtowels
DMC 'Hermina' or equivalent 4-ply cotton
crochet hook No 2.50

Clockwise from bottom: Lotus bath towel edging (page 58), Sheena hand towel edging (page 60) and Petite face washer edging (page 66)

Alison

1st row: 1dc into each st of previous row, turn.
2nd row: 1dc in 1st dc, 4ch, 1dc in same st, 5dc, ★ 4ch, 1dc in same place as last dc, 5dc; repeat from ★ ending with 4ch, 1dc in same st, 1dc, 1ch, turn.
3rd row: work into ch lp: ★ 2dc 1p 2dc, 2ch, into next lp work: (1dbl tr 1ch) 3 times, (1dbl tr 1p 1dbl tr 1ch) 3 times, 1dbl tr, 2ch; repeat from ★ to end of row, close with dc in turning ch.
4th row: 1dc into picot, ★ (1tr, 2ch) 3 times, (1tr, 4ch, 1tr, 2ch) 3 times, 1tr; repeat from ★ to end of row, 1dc in last picot, 1tr in turning ch, 1ch, turn.
5th row: ★ work into first 3sps of fan: 2dc 1p 2dc, in next sp 3dc 1p 3dc, in each of next 3sps: 2dc 1p 2dc, 1dc in 4ch lp; repeat from ★ to end of row, close with 2dc.
Fasten off.

3ch 1tr in next sp; repeat from ★ to end of rnd, turn.
4th row: sl st into first sp, 1dc in same sp, ★ (3dbl tr cl 3ch 3dbl tr cl) 5 times, 1dc in sp between fans; repeat from ★ to end of row, 1dc in last sp, sl st along edge to first row, turn.
5th row: work 4 picots to first sp of fan, 9 picots around each fan, 4 picots along other side of edge. Close with sl st.
Fasten off.

Toni

1st row: 2ch, 1tr in first dc, ★ skip 2dc, 1tr 3ch 1tr in next dc; repeat from ★ to end of row, turn.
2nd row: sl st into first sp, (1tr 3ch 1tr in next sp) twice, ★ skip 1sp, into next sp work: (3dbl tr cl 3ch) 3 times, 3dbl tr cl, skip 1sp, (1tr 3ch 1tr) 3 times; repeat from ★ to end of rnd, ending with (1tr 3ch 1tr) twice, turn.
3rd row: sl st into first sp, 5ch, 1tr in same sp, ★ skip 1sp, in each of 3ch sps between dbl tr cl work: 3dbl tr cl 3ch 3dbl tr cl divided by 3ch, skip 1sp, 1tr

Sheena

1st row: 4tr, 2ch, ★ skip 2dc, 1tr, skip 3dc, 7dbl tr in next st, skip 3dc, 1tr, skip 2dc, 9tr, skip 3dc, 1tr; repeat from ★ to end of row, ending with 4tr, 3ch, turn.
2nd row: 1tr in second tr, ★ skip 2tr and sp, (1dbl tr 2ch) 6 times, 1dbl tr, skip sp and 2tr, 5tr; repeat from

Clockwise from left: Toni handtowel edging (page 60), Scallops face washer edging (page 66) and Wheat bathtowel edging (page 59)   Below: Alison handtowel edging (page 60) and Mimosa face washer edging (page 66)

From the top: Mignon, Babette and Chantal shelf edgings (page 67)

Maartje milkjug cover (page 71)

Elisabeth milkjug cover (page 69)

Nel milkjug cover (page 71)

Janny milkjug cover (page 70)

63

Clockwise from top: Sweetheart basket (page 75), small and large bowls (page 74) and sauce bottle cover (page 73) with inset, vinegar bottle cover (page 73)

Clockwise from bottom: Wheat bathtowel edging (page 59), Toni handtowel edging (page 60) and Scallops face washer (page 66)

★ to end of row ending with 2tr, 5ch, turn.
3rd row: ★ (3dbl tr cl in sp, 3ch) 5 times, 3dbl tr cl, 2ch, 1tr in 3rd tr, 2ch; repeat from ★ to end of row, close with 2ch, 1tr.
4th row: sl st along side to 1st row, turn, (4ch, 1dc in next sp) 9 times, skip 1tr, 1dc in next sp, (4ch, 1dc) 6 times, skip 1tr; repeat from ★ to end of row, work 3 more lps along side edge, close with 1dc, 1ch, turn.
5th row: 1dc in first lp, 1dc 1htr 1tr 1htr 1dc in each 4ch lp till only one lp remains, 1dc in last lp, close with sl st.
Fasten off.

Kathy

1st row: 1tr in each st, 3ch, turn.
2nd row: ★ (2ch, skip 2tr, 1tr) 4 times, 3ch, skip 4tr, 1tr 2ch 1dbl tr 2ch 1tr in next st, skip 4tr, 1tr; repeat from ★ to end of row, end with (2ch, 1tr) 4 times, 3ch, turn.
3rd row: (1tr, 2ch) 3 times, 1tr, ★ 6tr in 2ch sp, 1tr in dbl tr, 6tr in next 2ch sp, skip 3ch sp, (1tr, 2ch) 4 times, 1tr; repeat from ★ to end of row, end with (1tr, 2ch) 4 times, 1tr, turn.
4th row: sl st over first sp and into tr, 5ch, 1tr, 2ch, 1tr, ★ in first tr of fan work 1tr 3ch 1tr, skip 2tr, (2ch, 1tr) twice, 1tr in same place as last tr, (2ch, 1tr) twice, 2ch, 1tr in same place as last tr, skip 2sps, (1tr, 2ch) twice, 1tr; repeat from ★ to end of row, turn.
5th row: sl st over next sp and into tr, 3ch, work 4tr in each of next 7 sps of fan, 1tr in 2nd tr; repeat from ★ to end of row, sl st along side edge to first row, 3ch, turn.
6th row: 6 picots to beginning of fan, ★ (1p, skip 2tr) 8 times, 1p, 1p between fans; repeat from ★ to end of row, 6p along side edge, close with sl st.
Fasten off.

FACE WASHER EDGINGS

Alison hand towel edging (page 60) and Mimosa face washer edging (this page)

All face washer edgings begin with 1 round of 1dc, 1ch, close with sl st. Use a smaller size crochet hook for this first round, as it moves more easily through the material and won't make holes.

Materials: face washer
         DMC 'Hermina' or equivalent 4-ply cotton
         crochet hook No 2.50

Scallops

1st rnd: 1dc in first st, ★ skip 2sts, 5tr in next st, skip 2sts, 1dc in next st; repeat from ★ taking care to space the scallops evenly and ease around corners. Close with sl st.
Fasten off.

Petite

1st rnd: ★ 1dc, 4ch, skip 2sts; repeat from ★ to end of rnd, close with sl st. You will need an even number of loops.
2nd rnd: sl st into first lp, 3ch, (for first tr), 2tr 4ch 1dc in base of st (picot made), 3tr in first lp, 1dc in next lp, ★ 3tr 1p 3tr in following lp; repeat from ★ to end of rnd, close with sl st.
Fasten off.

Petal

1st rnd: 1tr, ★ 2ch, skip 2sts, 1tr; repeat from ★ to end of rnd, close with sl st.
2nd rnd: ★ 1dc in first 2ch sp, 4ch, skip 1sp, in next 2ch sp work 3dbl tr cl 4ch 3dbl tr cl, 4ch, skip 1sp; repeat from ★ to end of rnd, close with sl st.
3rd rnd: sl st into first 4ch lp, 1dc in same lp, 4ch, 1dc in base of st (picot made), ★ 1dc in same 4ch lp, 1p, 1dc in next 4ch sp, 1p; repeat from ★ to end of rnd, close with sl st. Fasten off.

Mimosa

1st rnd: 1dc, ★ 3ch, skip 3sts, 1tr in each of next 3dc, 3ch, 1dbl tr in same place as last tr, 1dbl tr in each of next 2dc working the 3dbl tr into a cluster, 3ch, 1tr in same place as last dbl tr, 2tr, 3ch, skip 3sts, 1dc in next dc; repeat from ★ to end of rnd, close with sl st.
2nd rnd: sl st into 3ch lp, 1dc in same lp, 3ch, 1dc in base of 3ch (picot made), ★ 1dc in next 3ch sp, 1p, 1dc in same sp, 1p; repeat from ★ to end of rnd, close with sl st.
Fasten off.

SHELF EDGINGS

Mignon
Shelf edging in fillet crochet 12 cm (5") wide

Materials: 1 x 50 g ball DMC 'Hermina' or
equivalent 4-ply cotton
crochet hook No 2

Commence with 15ch.
1st row: 1tr in 4th ch from hook, 6tr, 1sp, 4tr, 3ch, turn.
2nd row: 3tr, 1sp, 7tr, 8ch, turn.
3rd row: skip 3ch, 6tr, 3sps, 4tr, 3ch, turn.
4th row: 3tr, 3sps, 7tr, 8ch, turn.
5th row: skip 3ch, 6tr, 2sps, 7tr, 1sp, 4tr, 3ch, turn.
6th row: 3tr, 1sp, 7tr, 2sps, 7tr, 8ch, turn.
7th row: skip 3ch, 6tr, 2sps, 7tr, 3sps, 4tr, 3ch, turn.
8th row: 3tr, 3sps, 7tr, 2sps, 7tr, 8ch, turn.
9th row: skip 3ch, 6tr, 2sps, 7tr, 2sps, 7tr, 1sp, 4tr, 3ch, turn.
10th row: 3tr, 1sp, 7tr, (2sps, 7tr) twice, 1ch, turn.
11th row: sl st over first 7sts, 3ch, 6tr, 2sps, 7tr, 3sps, 4tr, 3ch, turn.
12th row: 3tr, 3sps, 7tr, 2sps, 7tr, 1ch, turn.
13th row: sl st over first 7sts, 3ch, 6tr, 2sps, 7tr, 1sp, 4tr, 3ch, turn.
14th row: 3tr, 1sp, 7tr, 2sps, 7tr, 1ch, turn.
15th row: sl st over first 7sts, 3ch, 6tr, 3sps, 4tr, 3ch, turn.
16th row: 3tr, 3sps, 7tr, 1ch, turn.
17th row: sl st over first 7sts, 3ch, 6tr, 1sp, 4tr, 3ch, turn.
Repeat from 2nd row for length required.
Fasten off.

Babette
Shelf edging in fillet crochet, 15 cm (6") wide
Materials: 1 x 50 g ball DMC 'Hermina' or
equivalent 4-ply cotton
crochet hook No 2
Commence with 36ch.
1st row: 1tr in 4th ch from hook, 33tr, 3ch, turn (34tr).
2nd row: 3tr, 2sps, 7tr, 5sps, 4tr, 3ch, turn.
3rd row: 3tr, 5sps, 7tr, 2sps, 4tr, 5ch, turn.
4th row: 3tr, 10sps, 4tr, 3ch, turn.
5th row: 3tr, 10sps, 4tr, 5ch, turn.

From the top: Mignon, Babette and Chantal shelf edgings

6th row: 3tr, 11sps, 4tr, 3ch, turn.
7th row: 3tr, 4sps, 13tr, 3sps, 4tr, 5ch, turn.
8th row: 3tr, 3sps, 4tr, 1 bar, 1 lacet, 4tr, 3sps, 4tr, 3ch, turn.*9th row*: 3tr, 2sps, 4tr, 1sp, 1 bar, 1 lacet, 1sp, 4tr, 2sps, 4tr, 5ch, turn.
10th row: 3tr, 2sps, 4tr, (1 lacet, 1 bar) twice, 4tr, 1sp, 4tr, 3ch, turn.
11th row: 3tr, 1sp, 4tr, 1 lacet, 1sp, 7tr, 1sp, 1 bar, 4tr, 2sps, 4tr, 3ch, turn.
12th row: 3tr, 2sps, 4tr, 1 lacet, 1sp, 7tr, 1sp, 4tr, 1sp, 4tr, 3ch, turn.
13th row: 3tr, 1sp, 4tr, (1 lacet, 1 bar) twice, 4tr, 2sps, 4tr, 1ch, turn.
14th row: sl st over first 4tr, 3ch, 3tr, 2sps, 4tr, 1sp, 1 bar, 1 lacet, 1sp, 4tr, 2sps, 4tr, 3ch, turn.
15th row: 3tr, 3sps, 4tr, 1 bar, 1 lacet, 4tr, 3sps, 4tr, 2ch, turn.
16th row: sl st over 4tr, 3ch, 3tr, 3sps, 13tr, 4sps, 4tr, 3ch, turn.
17th row: 3tr, 11sps, 4tr, 1ch, turn.
18th row: sl st over 4tr, 3ch, 3tr, 10sps, 4tr, 3ch, turn.
19th row: 3tr, 10sps, 4tr, 1ch, turn.
20th row: sl st over 4tr, 3ch, 3tr, 2sps, 7tr, 5sps, 4tr, 3ch, turn.
Repeat from 3rd row for length required.
Repeat rows 2 and 1 once more.
Fasten off.

Chantal

Shelf edging in fillet crochet, 14 cm (5½") wide

Materials: 1 x 50 g ball DMC 'Hermina or
equivalent 4-ply cotton
crochet hook No 2

Commence with 45ch (42 + 3)
1st row: 1tr in 4th ch from hook, 42tr, 3ch, turn
(43tr).
2nd row: 3tr, (5sps, 4tr) twice, 1sp, 2ch, 1tr in same
place as last tr, 3ch, turn.
3rd row: 4tr, 1sp, 4tr, 4sps, 4tr, 5ch, 4tr, 4sps, 4tr, 3ch,
turn.
4th row: 3tr, 3sps, 4tr, 4ch, 1dc in centre of 5ch lp,
4ch, 4tr, 3sps, 4tr, 1sp, 2ch, 1tr in same place as last tr,
3ch, turn.
5th row: 4tr, 1sp, 4tr, 2sps, 4tr, 5ch, 3dc, 5ch, 4tr, 2sps,
4tr, 3ch, turn.
6th row: 3tr, 1sp, 4tr, 6ch, 5dc, 6ch, 4tr, 1sp, 4tr, 1sp,
2ch, 1tr in same place as last tr, 3ch, turn.
7th row: 4tr, 1sp, 4tr, 2sps, 4tr, 5ch, 3dc, 5ch,
4tr, 2sps, 4tr, 3ch, turn.
8th row: 3tr, 3sps, 4tr, 5ch, 1dc, 5ch, 4tr, 3sps, 4tr,
1sp, 2ch, 1tr in same place as last tr, 3ch, turn.
9th row: 4tr, 1sp, 4tr, 4sps, 4tr, 2ch, 4tr, 4sps, 4tr, 3ch,
turn.
Repeat rows 2-9 for length required.
Repeat row 1.
Fasten off.

MILKJUG COVERS

Does anyone still use milk jug covers, you may ask. They look delightfully old-fashioned and we know that our grandmothers used them. But then: think. Are they not very practical? Many people are rediscovering the usefulness of these dainty covers. I have seen them used on sugar bowls, and I am sure that you can think of many other uses.

Elisabeth

Round beaded cover, 24 cm (9½")

Materials: 1 x 20g ball DMC No 40
crochet hook No 0.75
20 glass beads

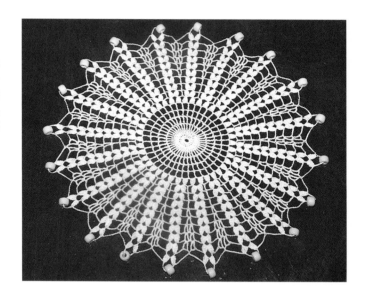

Thread the 20 beads onto your ball of cotton.
Commence with 6ch, close with sl st to form a ring.
1st rnd: 3ch (for first tr), 19tr in ring, close with sl st in 3rd of 3ch.
2nd rnd: 3ch, 1tr in same place as last sl st, 2tr in each tr, close with sl st.
3rd rnd: 5ch, ★ 1dbl tr in next tr, 1ch; repeat from ★ to end of rnd, close with sl st in 4th of 5ch.
4th and 5th rnds: 6ch, ★ 1dbl tr in next dbl tr, 2ch; repeat from ★ to end of rnd, close with sl st in 4th of 6ch.
6th rnd: 7ch, ★ 1dbl tr in next dbl tr, 3ch; repeat from ★ to end of rnd, close with sl st in 4th of 7ch.
7th rnd: sl st into next sp, 4ch 3dbl tr cl in same sp, ★ 4ch, 4dbl tr cl in next sp; repeat from ★ to end of rnd, close with sl st in top of first cl.
8th rnd: sl st in next lp, 4ch 3dbl tr cl in same sp, ★ 4ch, 4dbl tr cl in same sp, 2ch, 1dbl tr in next sp, 2ch, 4dbl tr cl in next lp; repeat from ★ omitting cl at end of last repeat, close with sl st in top of first cl.
9th rnd: sl st in next lp, 4ch 3dbl tr cl in same lp, ★ 4ch, 4dbl tr cl in same lp, 3ch, 1tr in next dbl tr, 3ch, 4dbl tr cl in next 4ch lp; repeat from ★ omitting cl at end of last repeat, close with sl st in top of first cl.
10th rnd: sl st in next lp, 4ch 3dbl tr cl in same lp, ★ 4ch, 4dbl tr cl in same lp, 4ch, 1tr in next tr, 4ch, 4dbl tr cl in next 4ch lp; repeat from ★ to end of rnd,

omitting cl at end of last repeat, close with sl st in top of first cl.
11th rnd: sl st in next lp, 4ch 3dbl tr cl in same lp, ★ 4ch, 4dbl tr cl in same lp, 4ch, in next tr work 1tr 2ch 1tr, 4ch, 4dbl tr cl in next 4ch lp; repeat from ★ omitting cl at end of last repeat, close with sl st in top of first cl.
12th rnd: sl st in next lp, 4ch 3dbl tr cl in same lp, ★ 4ch, 4dbl tr cl in same lp, in next 2ch sp work 1dbl tr 2ch 1dbl tr, 4ch, skip next 4ch sp, 4dbl tr cl in next 4ch lp; repeat from ★ omitting cl at end of last repeat, close with sl st in top of first cl.
13th rnd: sl st in next lp, 4ch 3dbl tr cl in same lp, ★ 4ch, 4dbl tr cl in same lp, 4ch, (in next dbl tr work 1dbl tr 2ch 1dbl tr) twice, 4ch, 4dbl tr cl in next 4ch lp; repeat from ★ omitting cl at end of last repeat, close with sl st in top of first cl.
14th rnd: sl st in next lp, 4ch 3dbl tr cl in same lp, ★ 4ch, 4dbl tr cl in same lp, 5ch, (in next 2ch sp work 1dbl tr 2ch 1dbl tr) twice, 5ch, 4dbl tr cl in next 4ch lp; repeat from ★ omitting cl at end of last repeat, close with sl st in top of first cl.
15th rnd: sl st in next lp, 4ch 3dbl tr cl in same lp, ★ 4ch, 3dbl tr cl in same lp, 5ch, in next 2ch sp work 1dbl tr 2ch 1dbl tr, 1ch, in next 2ch sp work 1dbl tr 2ch 1dbl tr, 5ch, 4dbl tr cl in next 4ch lp; repeat from ★ omitting cl at end of last repeat, close with sl st in top of first cl.

16th rnd: sl st in next lp, 4ch 3dbl tr cl in same lp, ★ 6ch, 4dbl tr cl in same lp, 5ch, in next 2ch sp work 1dbl tr 2ch 1dbl tr, 2ch, skip next sp, in next 2ch sp work 1dbl tr 2ch 1dbl tr, 5ch, 4dbl tr cl in next lp; repeat from ★ omitting cl at end of last repeat, close with sl st in top of first cl.

17th rnd: sl st in next lp, 4ch, 3dbl tr cl in same lp, ★ 10ch, thread bead over ch lp, 4dbl tr cl in same lp, 8ch, skip next 2sps, 1dc in 2ch lp, 8ch, 4dbl tr cl in 6ch lp; repeat from ★ omitting cl at end of last repeat, close with sl st in top of first cl.
Fasten off.

Janny
Round beaded cover, 21 cm (8¼")

Materials: 1 x 20 g ball DMC No 40
                    crochet hook No 0.75
                    21 glass beads

Thread 21 beads onto your ball of cotton.
Commence with 6ch, close with sl st to form a ring.
1st rnd: 6ch, ★ 1tr, 3ch; repeat from ★ 4 more times, sl st in 3rd of 6ch.
2nd rnd: in each sp work 1dc 1htr 3tr 1htr and 1dc (6 petals), close with sl st.
3rd rnd: ★ 5ch, 1dc in next tr of first rnd inserting

hook from the back; repeat from ★ ending with 5ch, close with sl st.
4th rnd: in each sp work 1dc 1htr 5tr 1htr and 1dc.
5th rnd: ★ 7ch, 1dc in next dc of round before last, inserting hook from the back; repeat from ★ ending with 7ch, close with sl st.
6th rnd: in sp work 1dc 1htr 7tr 1htr and 1dc, sl st in first dc.
7th rnd: 7ch, 1tr in same sp, 4ch, ★ 1tr 4ch 1tr between each petal, 4ch; repeat from ★ close with sl st in 4th of 7ch.
8th rnd: 3ch, 6tr in 4ch lp, ★ 1tr in tr, 6tr in 4ch lp; repeat from ★ close with sl st.
9th rnd: 3ch, 1tr in each of next 5tr, ★ 5ch, skip 1tr, 1tr in each of next 6tr; repeat from ★ omitting last 6tr, close with sl st in 3rd of 3ch.
10th rnd: ★ 1tr in each of next 6tr, (3ch, 1dc in 5ch lp, 3ch, skip 1tr) (lacet made); repeat from ★ close with sl st.
11th rnd: 3ch, 1tr in each of next 5tr, ★ 6ch, skip 1tr, 1tr in each of next 6tr; repeat from ★ omitting last 6tr, close with sl st.
12th rnd: 3ch, 1tr in each of next 5tr, ★ 4ch, 1dc in centre of 6ch bar, 4ch (lacet made), skip 1tr, 1tr in each of next 6tr; repeat from ★ omitting last 6tr, close with sl st.
13th rnd: as 9th rnd, but work 8ch bar instead of 6ch.
14th rnd: 3ch, 1tr in each of next 5tr, ★ 5ch, 1tr in centre of 8ch bar, 5ch, skip 1tr, 1tr in each of next 6tr; repeat from ★ to end of rnd, omitting last 6tr, close with sl st.
15th rnd: 3ch, 1tr in each of next 5tr, ★ 3ch lacet in first bar, 1tr in next tr, 3ch lacet in next bar, skip 1tr, 1tr in each of next 6tr; repeat from ★ close with sl st.
16th rnd: sl st to next tr, 3ch, 1tr in each of next 4tr, ★ 7ch, 1tr in next tr, 7ch, skip 1tr, 1tr in each of next 5tr; repeat from ★ to end of rnd, close with sl st.
17th rnd: sl st to next tr, 3ch, 1tr in each of next 3tr, ★ 4ch lacet in 7ch bar, 1tr in next tr, 4ch lacet, skip 1tr, 1tr in each of next 4tr; repeat from ★ to end of rnd, omitting last 4tr, close with sl st.
18th rnd: sl st to next tr, 3ch, 1tr in each of next 2tr, ★ 9ch, 1tr in next tr, 9ch, skip 1tr, 1tr in each of next 3tr; repeat from ★ to end of rnd, omitting last 3tr, close with sl st.
19th rnd: sl st to next tr, 3ch, 1tr in tr, ★ 5ch lacet in 9ch bar, 1tr in next tr, 5ch lacet in 9ch bar, 1tr in each of next 2tr; repeat from ★ to end of rnd, omitting last 2tr, close with sl st.
20th rnd: sl st to next tr, 3ch (for first tr), ★ 11ch, 1tr in tr, 11ch, 1tr in tr; repeat from ★ close with sl st in 4th of first 14ch.
21st rnd: ★ (1tr, 3ch) 3 times in 11ch lp, 3ch, (1tr, 3ch) 3 times in next 11ch lp; repeat from ★ close with sl st in first tr.

22nd rnd: 1dc in first tr, ★ 6ch, 1dc in next tr; repeat from ★ to end of rnd, working last lp 2ch 1tr in first dc.
23rd rnd: as 22nd rnd from ★.
24th rnd: ★ 7ch, 1dc in centre of next lp; repeat from ★ working last lp 2ch 1tr in first dc.
25th rnd: ★ 7ch, thread 1 bead over ch lp, 1dc in centre of next lp, (7ch, 1dc in centre of next lp) 6 times; repeat from ★ close with sl st.
Fasten off.

Maartje

Round beaded cover, 21 cm (8¼")

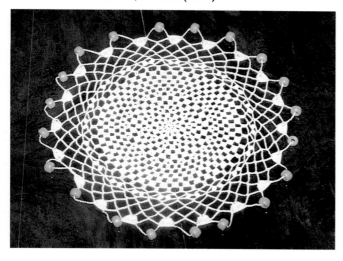

Materials: 1 x 20 g ball DMC No 40
crochet hook No 0.75
20 glass beads

Thread beads onto your ball of crochet cotton.
Commence with 6ch, close with sl st to form a ring.
1st rnd: 1tr, 1ch (10 times).
2nd rnd: sl st into ch sp, ★ 2tr, 2ch; repeat from ★ to end of rnd, close with sl st.
3rd rnd: sl st into 2ch sp, ★ 3tr, 3ch; repeat from ★ close with sl st.
4th rnd: sl st into 3ch sp, ★ 2tr 2ch 2tr in each 3ch sp, 2ch; repeat from ★ close with sl st.
5th rnd: sl st into 3ch sp, ★ 2tr in same sp, 2ch, 3tr in next sp; repeat from ★ close with sl st.
6th rnd: sl st into 2ch sp, ★ 3tr in each sp, 3ch; repeat from ★ close with sl st.
7th rnd: sl st into 3ch sp, ★ 4tr in each 3ch sp, 3ch; repeat from ★ close with sl st.
8th rnd: sl st into 3ch sp, ★ 2tr 2ch 2tr in each sp,

2ch; repeat from ★ close with sl st.
9th rnd: sl st into 2ch sp, ★ 2tr 2ch in each sp; repeat from ★ close with sl st.
10th rnd: sl st into 2ch sp, ★ 2tr 3ch in each sp; repeat from ★ close with sl st.
11th rnd: sl st into 3ch sp, ★ 3tr 2ch in each sp; repeat from ★ close with sl st.
12th rnd: sl st into 2ch sp, ★ 3tr 3ch in each sp; repeat from ★ close with sl st.
13th rnd: sl st into 3ch sp, ★ 4tr 3ch in each sp; repeat from ★ close with sl st.
14th rnd: sl st over tr into 3ch sp, ★ 2tr in 3ch sp, 5ch; repeat from ★ to end of rnd, working last lp 2ch 1tr in top of tr.
15th rnd: ★ 7ch, 1dc in centre of each 5ch lp; repeat from ★ to end of rnd, close with 3ch 1tr as last rnd.
16th rnd: ★ 3ch, in next 5ch lp work 3tr cl 5ch 3tr cl, 3ch, 1dc in next lp; repeat from ★ close with sl st.
17th rnd: ★ 8ch, 1dc in 5ch lp between cls, 8ch, 1dc in dc; repeat from ★ to end of rnd, work last lp 3ch 1dbl tr in first st.
18th rnd: ★ 9ch, 1dc in centre of 8ch lp; repeat from ★ to end of rnd, close with 4ch 1dbl tr.
19th rnd: ★ 10ch, 1dc in centre of each 9ch lp; repeat from ★ to end of rnd, close with 4ch 1tr in tr.
20th rnd: ★ 5ch, 7dbl tr in centre ch of 9ch lp, 1dc in next lp; repeat from ★ to end of rnd, close with sl st.
21st rnd: sl st to 7dbl tr, ★ 1dc in each dbl tr, 15ch, thread bead over; repeat from ★ close with sl st.
Fasten off.

Nel

Round beaded cover, 22 cm (8½")

Materials: 1 x 20 g ball DMC No 40
crochet hook No 0.75
12 glass beads

Thread beads onto your ball of crochet cotton.
Commence with 8ch, close with sl st to form a ring.
1st rnd: 3ch (for first tr), 4ch, (1tr, 4ch) 5 times (6sps made); close with sl st in 3rd of 3ch.
2nd rnd: sl st into 4ch lp, ★ 1tr 2ch 1tr in each 4ch lp, 3ch; repeat from ★ close with sl st in first tr.
3rd rnd: ★ 1tr 2ch 1tr in first tr, 2ch, 1tr 2ch 1tr in next tr, 3ch; repeat from ★ close with sl st.
4th rnd: ★ 1tr 2ch 1tr in first tr, 2ch, 1tr in next tr, 1ch, 1tr in next tr, 2ch, 1tr 2ch 1tr in next tr, 2ch; repeat from ★ close with sl st.
5th rnd: ★ 1tr 2ch 1tr in first tr, (2ch 1tr in next tr)

twice, 2ch, (1tr, 2ch) twice, 1tr 2ch 1tr in next tr, 2ch; repeat from ★ close with sl st.

6th rnd: ★ 1tr 2ch 1tr in first tr, 2ch, (1tr in next tr, 5ch, 1tr in next tr, 2ch) twice, 1tr 2ch 1tr in next tr, 2ch; repeat from ★ close with sl st.

7th rnd: ★ 1tr 2ch 1tr in first tr, (2ch, 1tr) twice, 3ch, 1dc in centre of 5ch lp, 3ch, 1tr in tr, 1tr in sp, 1tr in tr, 3ch, 1dc in centre of 5ch lp, 3ch, (1tr in tr, 2ch) twice, 1tr 2ch 1tr in next tr, 2ch; repeat from ★ close with sl st.

8th rnd: ★ 1tr 2ch 1tr in first tr, (2ch, 1tr) 3 times, 5ch, 1tr in next tr, 1ch, skip 1tr, 1tr in next tr, 5ch, (1tr, 2ch) 3 times, 1tr 2ch 1tr in next tr, 2ch; repeat from ★ close with sl st.

9th rnd: ★ 1tr 2ch 1tr in first tr, (2ch, 1tr) 4 times, 3ch, 1dc in centre of 5ch lp, 3ch, 1tr in tr, 1tr in sp, 1tr in tr, 3ch, 1dc in centre of 5ch lp, 3ch, (1tr, 2ch) 4 times, 1tr 2ch 1tr in next tr, 1ch; repeat from ★ close with sl st.

10th rnd: ★ 1tr 2ch 1tr in first tr, (2ch, 1tr) 5 times, 5ch, 1tr in tr, 1ch, skip 1tr, 1tr in tr, 5ch, (1tr, 2ch) 5 times, 1tr 2ch 1tr in next tr, 1ch; repeat from ★ close with sl st.

11th rnd: ★ 1tr 2ch 1tr in first tr, (2ch, 1tr) 6 times, 3ch, 1dc in centre of 5ch lp, 3ch, 1tr in tr, 1tr in sp, 1tr in tr, 3ch, 1dc in centre of 5ch lp, 3ch, (1tr, 2ch) 6 times, 1tr 2ch 1tr in next tr, 1ch; repeat from ★ close with sl st.

12th rnd: 8ch, skip 2tr, 1tr in next tr, 2ch, ★ 1tr in next tr, 5ch, skip 1tr, 1tr in next tr, 2ch, (1tr in next tr, 5ch, 1tr in next tr 2ch) twice, 1tr in next tr, 5ch, skip 1tr, 1tr in next tr, 2ch, 1tr in next tr, skip 2tr, 1tr in next tr, 2ch; repeat from ★ close with sl st in 4th of 8ch.

13th rnd: 6ch, 1dc in centre of 5ch lp, 3ch, 1tr in tr, 1tr in sp, 1tr in tr, ★ 3ch, 1dc in centre of 5ch lp, 3ch, 1tr in tr, 1tr in sp, 1tr in tr; repeat from ★ close with sl st in 4th of 6ch.

14th rnd: 9ch, 1tr in tr, 2ch, skip 1tr, 1tr in tr, ★ 6ch, 1tr in tr, 2ch, skip 1tr, 1tr in tr; repeat from ★ close with sl st in 4th of 9ch.

15th rnd: 6ch, 1dc in centre of 6ch lp, 3ch, 1tr in tr, 1tr in sp, 1tr in tr, ★ 3ch, 1dc in centre of 6ch lp, 3ch, 1tr in tr, 1tr in sp, 1tr in tr; repeat from ★ close with sl st in 4th of 6ch.

16th rnd: 10ch, 1tr in tr, 2ch, skip 1tr, 1tr in tr, ★ 7ch, 1tr in tr, 2ch, skip 1tr, 1tr in tr; repeat from ★ close with sl st in 4th of 10ch.

17th rnd: 7ch, 1dc in centre of 7ch lp, 4ch, 1tr in tr, 1tr in sp, 1tr in tr, ★ 4ch, 1dc in centre of 7ch lp, 4ch, 1tr in tr, 1tr in sp, 1tr in tr; repeat from ★ close with sl st in 4th of 7ch.

18th rnd: 11ch, 1tr in tr, 2ch, skip 1tr, 1tr in tr, ★ 8ch, 1tr in tr, 2ch, skip 1tr, 1tr in tr; repeat from ★ close with 4ch 1dbl tr in 4th of 11ch.

19th rnd: ★ (12ch, 1dc in centre of 8ch lp) twice, 12ch, thread bead over, 1dc in centre of next 8ch lp; repeat from ★ close with sl st.

Fasten off.

KITCHEN COVERS

Vinegar or Oil Bottle Cover

Bottle cover in trellis and fan stitch, 12 cm (5") high

Materials: 1 x 20 g ball DMC No 40
                  crochet hooks Nos 0.75 and 1.00
                  2 glass beads

Using No 0.75 hook, commence with 82ch, close with sl st to form a circle.
1st rnd: ★ 5ch, skip 3ch, 1dc in next ch; repeat from ★ close last lp with 2ch, 1tr in 1st st (20lps).
2nd rnd: ★ (5ch, 1dc in next lp) twice, 5tr in dc, 1dc in next lp, 5tr in dc; repeat from ★ to end of rnd, close with sl st.
3rd rnd: sl st to centre of lp, 1dc in same lp, 5ch, 1dc in next lp, ★ (5ch, 1dc in centre of fan) twice, (5ch, 1dc in next lp) twice; repeat from ★ to end of rnd, close with 2ch, 1tr in 1st dc.
Repeat rows 2 and 3 five more times, then work 2nd rnd once more (7 fans high).
15th rnd: sl st to centre lp, 1dc in same lp, 4ch, 1dc in next lp, ★ (5ch, 1dc in next lp) 3 times, 4ch, 1dc in next lp; repeat from ★ to end of rnd working last lp 2ch, 1tr in first dc.
16th rnd: ★ (4ch, 1dc in next lp) twice, 5tr in dc, 1dc in next lp, 5tr in dc; repeat from ★ to end of rnd, close with sl st.

Repeat these 2 rounds 6 more times (or length required), turn, wrong side facing, dividing work for handle.
29th rnd: sl st over first fan, 1dc, 4ch, 1dc in centre of next fan, 5ch, 1dc in next lp, ★ 4ch, 1dc in next lp, (5ch, 1dc in next lp) 3 times; repeat from ★ to end of row ending with (5ch, 1dc) twice, last dc in same sp as first dc, 1ch, turn.
30th rnd: 1dc into first lp, 5tr in dc, 1dc in next lp, ★ (4ch, 1dc in next lp) twice, (5tr in dc, 1dc in next lp) twice; repeat from ★ to end of row ending with (5tr in dc, 1dc in next lp) once, turn.
31st rnd: 4ch, 1dc in fan, 5ch, 1dc in next lp, ★ 4ch, 1dc in next lp, (5ch, 1dc in next lp) 3 times; repeat from ★ to end of row, 1dc in last lp, 1ch, turn.
Repeat last 2 rows 2 more times, then 30th row once more.
Fasten off.
With right side facing connect thread to base of work.
1st rnd: work 4dc in each lp, close with sl st.
2nd rnd: word 1dc in each second dc.
Fasten off.
Using double thread and No 1.00 crochet hook, make a cord 40 cm (16") long. Thread through top of work, attach a glass bead at each end of cord, and fit cover over bottle.

Vinegar or oil bottle cover (left)

and Sauce bottle cover

Sauce Bottle Cover

Bottle cover in shell trellis stitch, 14 cm (5½") high

Materials: 1 x 20 g ball DMC No 40
                  Crochet hooks No 0.75 and 1.00
                  2 glass beads

Notes: The number of chain and treble stitches may have to be adjusted if your bottle is a different size. Use a multiple of 12tr.

Using No 0.75 crochet hook, commence with 96ch, close with sl st to form a circle.
1st rnd: 108tr in same circle.
2nd rnd: sl st into first tr, 5tr in same tr, skip 2tr,

1dc in next tr, 5ch, skip 4tr, 1dc in next tr, skip 2tr, ★ 5tr in next tr, skip 2tr, 1dc in next tr, 5ch, skip 5tr, 1dc in next tr, skip 2tr; repeat from ★ to end of rnd, close with sl st in 5tr grp.

3rd rnd: sl st to 3rd tr, 1dc in centre tr of shell, ★ 5ch, 1dc in centre of 5ch lp, 5ch, 1dc in centre of shell, 5ch, 1dc in centre of 5ch lp, 5ch; repeat from ★ to end of rnd, close with sl st.

4th rnd: sl st to centre of 5ch lp, 1dc, ★ 5tr in dc, 1dc in centre of 5ch lp, 5ch, 1dc in centre of next 5ch lp; repeat from ★ to end of rnd, close with sl st in dc.

5th rnd: sl st to centre of shell, 1dc, 5ch, 1dc in centre of 5ch lp, 5ch, ★ 1dc in centre of shell, 5ch, 1dc in centre of 5ch lp, 5ch; repeat from ★ to end of rnd, close with sl st.

6th rnd: sl st to centre of 5ch lp, ★ 5tr in dc, 1dc in centre of 5ch lp, 5ch, 1dc in centre of next 5ch lp; repeat from ★ to end of rnd, close with sl st.

Repeat rnds 3-6 for 8 cm (3") or length required.

Decreasing

1st rnd: sl st to centre of shell, 1dc, 4ch, 1dc in centre of 5ch lp, 4ch, ★ 1dc in shell, 4ch, 1dc in centre of 5ch lp, 4ch; repeat from ★ to end of rnd, close with sl st.

2nd rnd: sl st to centre of 4ch lp, ★ 5tr in dc, 1dc in centre of 4ch lp, 4ch, 1dc in centre of next 4ch lp; repeat from ★ to end of rnd, close with sl st.

Repeat these 2 rnds 4 times, then 1st rnd once more.
Repeat 1st rnd 3 more times, but with 3ch between.

15th rnd: sl st into 3ch lp, 5ch, ★ 1tr in next lp, 2ch; repeat from ★ to end of rnd, close with sl st in 3rd of 5ch.

16th rnd: sl st into 2ch lp, 3ch, ★ 1dc, 3ch; repeat from ★ to end of rnd, close with sl st.

17th rnd: sl st into 3ch lp, 1dc in same lp, ★ 3ch, 1dc in base of st (picot made) 1dc in same lp, 1dc in next lp; repeat from ★ to end of rnd, close with sl st.
Fasten off.

Attach cotton to base of work. Work 1dc between each tr.

Next rnd: (2dc, skip 1dc) to end of rnd, close with sl st.
Fasten off.

Using double cotton and a No 1.00 crochet hook work a 40 cm (16") chain cord.
Thread this cord through 15th rnd and tie into a bow. Finish cord with a glass bead on each end.

Bowls

These two bowls are made to the same pattern, using different weights of cotton.

Large Bowl
Stiffened crochet bowl 22 cm (8½") in diameter, 7 cm (2¾") high

Materials: 1 ball DMC Hermina or equivalent 4-ply crochet hook No 2

Small Bowl
Stiffened crochet bowl 10 cm (4") in diameter, 4 cm (1½") high

Materials: 1 x 20 g ball DMC No 40 crochet hook No 0.75

Commence with 5ch, close with sl st to form a ring.
1st rnd: 5ch, (1tr, 2ch) into ring 7 times, close with sl st in 3rd of 5ch.

2nd rnd: sl st into sp, 3ch, 4tr in same sp, ★ 5tr in next sp; repeat from ★ to end of rnd, close with sl st in top of 3rd ch.

3rd rnd: 3ch, 1tr in each of next 4tr, ★ 3ch, 1tr in each of next 5tr; repeat from ★ to end of rnd, ending with 3ch, close with sl st.

4th rnd: (1dc in each tr, 3dc in each ch sp) all around, sl st in first dc.

5th rnd: 6ch, ★ (skip 1dc, 1tr in next dc, 3ch) twice, skip 3dc, 1tr in next dc, 3ch; repeat from ★ to end of rnd ending with 3ch, close with sl st in 3rd of 6ch.

6th rnd: 3ch, ★ 3tr in sp, 1tr in tr; repeat from ★ to end of rnd omitting tr in tr, close with sl st.

7th rnd: 4ch, 4dbl tr in same place, ★ skip 3tr, 5dbl tr in next tr; repeat from ★ to end of rnd, close with sl st in top of 4ch.

8th rnd: leaving last lp of each dbl tr on hook, 4ch, 1dbl tr in each of next 4dbl tr, yrh, draw yarn through all lps to form a grp, ★ 6ch, 1grp over next 5dbl tr; repeat from ★ to end of rnd ending with 6ch, sl st in top of first grp.

9th rnd: sl st into sp, 3ch, 6tr in sp, 7tr in each sp to end, close with sl st.

10th rnd: 6ch, ★ skip 2tr, 1tr in next tr, 3ch; repeat from ★ to end of rnd, close with sl st in 3rd of 6ch ch (56 sps).

Turn

11th rnd: 3ch, ★ 3tr in sp, 1tr in next tr; repeat from ★ to end of rnd, omitting 1tr in tr, close with sl st.

12th rnd: 6ch, 1tr in same place, ★ (6ch, skip 7tr, 1tr in next tr) twice, 3ch, 1tr in next tr; repeat from ★ to end of rnd ending with 6ch, skip 7tr, 1tr in tr, 6ch, close with sl st in 3rd of 6ch.

13th rnd: sl st into sp, 4ch, 3dbl tr 2ch 1dbl tr 2ch 4 dbl tr in same space, ★ 3ch, 1dbl tr in next tr, 3ch, 4dbl tr 2ch 1dbl tr 2ch 4dbl tr in next 3ch sp; repeat from ★ to end of rnd ending with 3ch, close with sl st in top of 4ch.

14th rnd: sl st over 3dbl tr and in 4ch sp, 3dbl tr in same sp, 2ch, 1dbl tr in dbl tr, 2ch, 4dbl tr in next sp, ★ 2ch, 1dbl tr in dbl tr, 2ch, 4dbl tr in next 2ch sp, 2ch, 1dbl tr in dbl tr, 2ch, 4dbl tr in next sp; repeat from ★ to end of rnd ending with 2ch, 1dbl tr in dbl tr, 2ch, close with sl st.

15th rnd: sl st over 3dbl tr and into sp, 4ch, 3dbl tr in same sp, 3ch, 1dbl tr in dbl tr, 3ch, 4dbl tr in next sp, ★ 1ch, 1dbl tr in next dbl tr, 1ch, 4dbl tr in next 2ch sp, 3ch, 1dbl tr in dbl tr, 3ch, 4dbl tr in next sp; repeat from ★ to end of rnd ending with 1ch, close with sl st.

16th rnd: sl st over 3dbl tr and into sp, 4ch, 1dbl tr in same sp, 4ch, sl st in 4th ch from hook (picot made), 2dbl tr in same sp as last dbl tr, 1p, 2dbl tr in dbl tr, (1p, 2dbl tr) twice in next sp, ★ 2ch, 1dbl tr in dbl tr, 2ch, (2dbl tr, 1p) twice in next 3ch sp, 2dbl tr in dbl tr, (1p, 2dbl tr) twice in next sp; repeat from ★ to end of rnd ending with 2ch, 1dbl tr in dbl tr, 2ch, close with sl st.
Fasten off.
Make a sugar solution with 1 part boiling water, 1 part white granulated sugar, heat to dissolve sugar. Mixture must be clear. Dip crochet directly in cooled solution, and saturate material.
Mould wet crochet over a bowl of the right diameter, and leave to dry.

Sweetheart Basket

Stiffened crochet basket 19 cm (7½") high

Materials: 1 x 20 g ball DMC No 40
crochet hook No 0.75
ribbon for handle, 25 cm x 7 mm (10" x ¼")
ribbon for bow, 50 cm x 3 cm (20" x 1¼")

Commence with 7ch, close with sl st to form a ring.
1st rnd: 3ch (for first tr), 15tr, close with sl st (16 tr).
2nd rnd: 4ch, ★ 1tr in tr, 1ch; repeat from ★ to end of rnd, close with sl st in 3rd of 4ch.
3rd rnd: 3ch, 1tr in same place, 1tr in next ch, ★ 2tr in next tr, 1tr in sp; repeat from ★ to end of rnd, close with sl st (48tr).
4th rnd: 4ch (for first dbl tr), work 1dbl tr in the back lp of each tr; close with sl st (48dbl tr).
5th rnd: 1ch, 1dc in same place, ★ 4ch, skip 2dbl tr, 1dc in next dbl tr; repeat from ★ 15 times, 1ch, 1tr in 1st dc (last 4ch lp made) (16 4ch lps).
6th to 9th rnds: dc in joining lp, ★ 4ch, 1dc in next lp; repeat from ★ 15 times, 1ch, close with tr in first dc.
10th rnd: 4ch (for first dbl tr), 1dbl tr in same place, 2ch, ★ 2dbl tr in next 4ch lp, 2ch; repeat from ★ to end of rnd, close with sl st in top of 4ch.
11th and 12th rnds: 4ch, 1dbl tr in next dbl tr, 2ch, ★ 1dbl tr in each of next 2dbl tr, 2ch; repeat from ★ to end of rnd, close with sl st.
13th rnd: 4ch, 1dbl tr in next dbl tr, 3ch, ★ 1dbl tr in each of next 2dbl tr, 3ch; repeat from ★ to end of rnd, close with sl st.

14th rnd: 4ch, work 1dbl tr in each st till end of rnd, close with sl st (80dbl tr).

15th rnd: 7ch, (for first dbl tr and 3ch), ★ skip 1dbl tr, 1dbl tr in front lp of next dbl tr, 3ch; repeat from ★ to end of rnd, close with sl st in 4th of 7ch (40 3ch sps).

16th rnd: sl st into first 3ch sp, 1ch, 1dc in same 3ch sp, ★ 4ch, 1dc in next 3ch sp; repeat from ★ 39 times, 1ch, close with tr in first dc.

17th to 19th rnds: 1dc in joining lp, ★ 4ch, 1dc in next lp; repeat from ★ 39 times, 1ch, close with 1tr in first dc.

20th rnd: 4ch (for first dbl tr), 1dbl tr in same place, 4ch, ★ 2dbl tr in next 4ch lp, 4ch; repeat from ★ to end of rnd, close with sl st.

21st rnd: 3ch, 1tr in same place, 4ch, 1dc in base st (picot made), 2tr in next dbl tr, 1ch, 1dc in 4ch sp, 1ch, ★ 2tr in next dbl tr, 1p, 2tr in next dbl tr, 1ch, 1dc in 4ch sp, 1ch; repeat from ★ to end of rnd, close with sl st.

22nd rnd: sl st to first picot, 1ch, 1dc in same p, ★ 6ch, 1dc in next p; repeat from ★ to end of rnd, close with sl st.

23rd rnd: sl st in 6ch lp, 1ch, 8dc in same 6ch lp, ★ sl st in next 6ch lp, 1ch, 8dc in same 6ch lp; repeat from ★ to end of rnd, close with sl st.
Fasten off.

Base

Join in front lp of any tr from rnd 3.

1st rnd: 2ch (for first htr), work 1htr in front lp of each tr to end of rnd, close with sl st.
Fasten off.

Handle

Commence with 111ch.

1st row: 1dbl tr in 11th ch from hook, ★ 3ch, skip 3ch, 1dbl tr in next ch; repeat from ★ to end of row, 6ch, turn.

2nd row: 1dc in next dbl tr, ★ 6ch, 1dc in next dbl tr; repeat from ★ to end of row, 1ch, turn.

3rd row: 7dc in 6ch lp, ★ sl st in next 6ch lp, 1ch, 7dc in same 6ch lp; repeat from ★ to end of row.
Break off yarn.

4th and 5th rows: Join at corner of opposite end of handle. Repeat rows 2 and 3 along opposite end of handle.
Fasten off.

Blocking

Cover styrofoam cup with plastic wrap and turn upside down on pinning board. Dip basket in stiffening solution (as for bowl, page 75). Shape bottom of basket over cup. Spread out rim and pin flat to board. Pin basket to outside edge of cup. Dip handle in solution and pin flat.

When still very damp unpin basket and stand upright; do not remove cup. Cover half empty roll of paper towel with plastic wrap and lay across top of styrofoam cup.

Fold up sides of rim around paper towel and pin to hold.

Fold damp handle over edge of same paper towel, and leave to dry.

When dry, remove styrofoam cup. Thread 7 mm (¼") ribbon through spaces of handle. Using craft glue attach handle to basket. Make a bow with 3 cm (1¼") ribbon and attach with craft glue to basket.

A larger basket may be made by using thicker cotton.

LACE EDGINGS, INSERTIONS AND BRAIDS

This section includes beautiful laces, edgings and insertions, suitable as trimmings for all kinds of items including women's blouses and underwear, babies' and children's wear and household linen.

Our great grandmothers used handmade crochet lace for all these, and now, as we approach the end of the twentieth century, handmade crochet edgings, insertions and braids have renewed fashion possibilities. A century ago there were only cotton and linen, and the hard work involved in washing, starching and ironing. The modern woman would think twice before going back to the discomfort of starched linen. But now we have beautiful easycare drip-dry materials, and the hand crocheted finishing touches look just as delightful now as they did last century.

So trim your clothes or household linen with some easycare hard wearing crochet, or work some lace edged handkerchiefs. They will be worth the time and effort you put in.

Varying the thickness of yarn will give you different effects. I have mainly used No 20 and No 40 DMC threads for these laces, but for soft furnishing trims it would be better to use thick cotton, or even wool, for a chunky modern look.

Ribbon Threaded Edgings

Scallops

Commence with 14ch.

1st row: 1tr in 8th ch from hook, 2ch, skip 2ch, 1tr in next ch, 3ch, 1tr in same place, leave last 3ch of foundation row, 2ch, turn.

2nd row: 7tr in 3ch lp, 2ch, skip 2ch sp, 1tr in tr, 2tr, 1tr in turning ch, 5ch, turn.

3rd row: 1tr in 4th tr from hook, (2ch, 1tr) 8 times, 2ch, 1dc in last ch of foundation ch, 3ch, turn.

4th row: skip first sp, 1tr in next sp, (3ch, 1tr in next sp) 6 times, 3ch, 1tr in same sp as last tr, 2ch, skip 2ch sp, 1tr in tr and 3 more tr along sts that turned, 5ch, turn.

5th row: 1tr in 4th tr from hook, 2ch, skip 2ch sp, 1tr in first of 3ch lps, 3ch, 1tr in same sp, 3ch, turn.

6th row: as 2nd row.

7th row: as 3rd row, but instead of dc at end, 1dc in tr of previous scallop.

8th row: as 4th row.

Repeat from 5th row for length required.

Break off yarn.

Edge along bottom of scallops

Attach yarn in first sp, 1dc, ★ (4ch, 1dc in base st [picot made], 1dc in next sp) 5 times, 1dc in next sp; repeat from ★ to end of row, close with sl st. Fasten off.

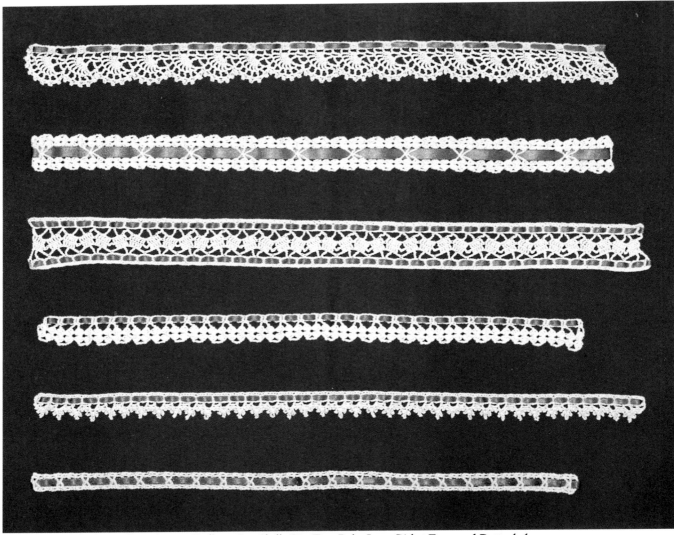

Ribbon threaded edgings: from the top, Scallops, Sea Shell, Zig-Zag, Baby Lace, Picket Fence and Buttonhole

Sea Shell

This versatile lace, threaded with ribbon, has many uses. A repeat of 8 patterns would make a lovely bookmark.

Commence with 10ch.
1st row: 2tr in 4th ch from hook, 2ch 3tr in same ch, 5ch, in last ch work 3tr 2ch 3tr, 3ch, turn.
2nd row: 3tr 2ch 3tr in shell, 5ch, 3tr 2ch 3tr in last shell, 3ch, turn.
3rd row: 3tr 2ch 3tr in shell, 4ch, 1dc over 5ch lps of previous 2 rows, 4ch, 3tr 2ch 3tr in last shell, 3ch, turn.
Repeat these 3 rows for length required.

Work last row as follows:
3tr 2ch 3tr in shell, 5ch, 3tr 2ch 3tr in last shell. Fasten off.

78

Zig-Zag

Make a chain for length required.

1st row: 1tr in 8th ch from hook, ★ 2ch, skip 2ch, 1tr in next ch; repeat from ★ to end of row, 1ch, turn.

2nd row: 1dc in first sp, 5ch, skip 1sp, 1dbl tr in next sp, 5ch, 1dbl tr in same sp, 5ch, skip 1sp, 1dc in next sp; repeat from ★ to end of row.

3rd row: sl st to 4th ch, 3ch, 1tr in next ch, 1tr in dbl tr, ★ in next 5ch lp work 3tr 5ch 3tr, 1tr in dbl tr, 2tr in next 2ch, skip 3ch 1dc and 3ch, 2tr, 1tr in dbl tr; repeat from ★ to end of row.

4th row: ★ sl st over tr, 1tr in each of next 5tr, 5ch, 1tr in each of next 5tr, skip 1tr; repeat from ★ to end of row.

5th row: 8ch, ★ 1dbl tr in 3rd tr, 5ch, 1dc in 5ch lp, 5ch, 1dbl tr in 3rd tr; repeat from ★ ending with 5ch, 1tr in turning ch, 5ch, turn.

6th row: 1tr in 3rd ch, 2ch, ★ 1tr in dbl tr, 2ch, 1tr in 3rd ch of 5ch 1p, 2ch, 1tr in dbl tr; repeat from ★ to end of row.

7th row: 1ch, ★ 2dc in 2ch lp, 1dc in tr; repeat from ★to end of row.

Work 7th row along cast-on edge.
Fasten off.

Baby Lace

Commence with 10ch.

1st row: 2tr in 7th ch from hook, 2tr in next ch, 3ch, 2tr in each of next 2ch, 5ch, turn.

2nd row: 4tr in 3ch lp, 3ch, 4tr in same lp, 5ch, turn.
Repeat these 2 rows for length required

Heading

1st row: ★ 5ch, 2dc in 4ch lp; repeat from ★ to end of row, 3ch, turn.

2nd row: 1tr, ★ 1ch, 2tr in centre of 5ch lp, 1ch, 2tr in dc; repeat from ★ to end of row, ending with 2tr in tr of last shell.
Fasten off.

Picket Fence

This dainty trim may be used for both children's clothes and adult garments.

Commence with 8ch.

1st row: 1tr in 8th ch from hook, 5ch, turn.

2nd row: skip first 2ch, 1tr in next ch, 5ch, turn.
Repeat 2nd row for length required omitting turning ch at end of last repeat and having an even number of spaces. Do not fasten off.

Edging

1st row: 1ch, 1dc in top of last tr, ★ 5ch, 1dc in base of same tr, 3ch, 1dc in top of next tr; repeat from ★ to end of row, work last dc in 3rd of turning ch, 1ch, turn.

2nd row: 1dc in first sp, 3ch, sl st in last dc (picot made), ★ 2dc in next 5ch lp, 5ch, sl st in last dc, 7ch, sl st in same dc, 5ch, sl st in same dc (triple picot made), 2dc in same lp, 1p, dc in next lp, 1p; repeat from ★ to end of row omitting 1dc at end of last repeat, close with sl st.

Heading

Work a row of dc along opposite side of lace, 3dc in each sp, close with sl st.

Buttonhole

This narrow lace can be used as it is or with ribbon threaded through the centre.

Commence with 11ch.

1st row: 1tr in 4th ch from hook, 2ch, skip 2ch, 1dc in next ch, 2ch, skip 2ch, 1tr in each of next 2ch, 3ch, turn.

2nd row: skip first tr, 1tr in next tr, 5ch, 1tr in next tr, 1tr in top of turning ch, 3ch, turn.

3rd row: skip first tr, 1tr in next tr, 2ch, 1dc in centre of 5ch lp, 2ch, 1tr in next tr, 1tr in turning ch, 3ch,
Repeat 2nd and 3rd rows for length required.
Fasten off.

Insertions

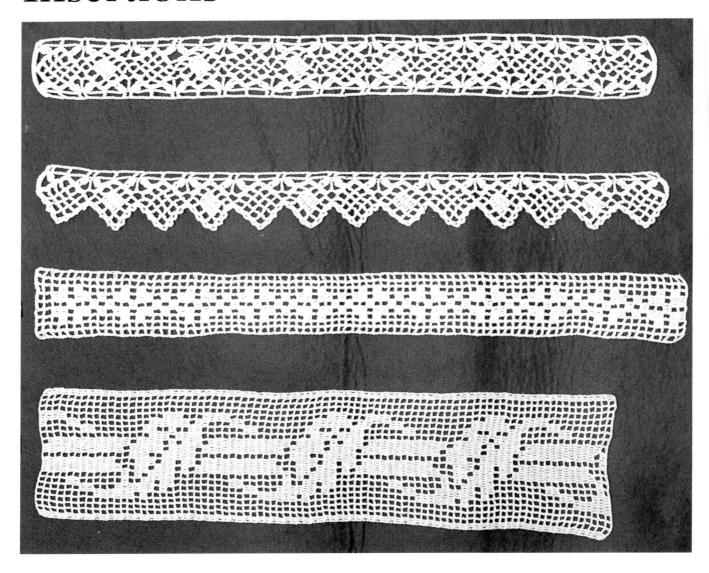

Insertions—from the top, Trellis, Trellis edging, Mosaic and Leaf and Bar

Trellis Insertion

Commence with 17ch.

1st row: 1tr in 8th ch from hook, (skip 2ch, 1tr in next ch) 3 times, 5ch, turn.

2nd and 3rd rows: skip first tr, (1tr in next tr, 2ch) 3 times, skip 2ch, 1tr in next ch, 5ch, turn.

4th row: Repeat 2nd row, 16ch, turn.

5th row: 1tr in 8th ch from hook, (2ch, skip 2ch, 1tr in next ch) twice, 2ch, 1tr in next tr, 5ch, turn.

6th row: skip 1st tr, 1tr in next tr, (2tr in next sp, 1tr in next tr) twice, 2ch, skip 2ch, 1tr in next ch, 5ch, turn.

7th row: skip 1st tr, 1tr in each of next 7tr, 2ch, skip 2ch, 1tr in next ch, 5ch, turn.

8th row: skip 1st tr, 1tr in next tr, (2ch, skip 2tr, 1tr in next tr) twice, 2ch, skip 2ch, 1tr in next ch, 16ch, turn.

9th row: as 5th row.

Repeat 2nd to 9th rows inclusive for length required, omitting last 5ch and turn.

Heading

Do not turn work.

1st rnd: 1ch, 2dc in same sp, *3dc in next sp, 1dc in next sp, 5ch, 1dc in first of 5ch (picot made), 1dc in same sp, 5dc in next sp, into next sp work 1dc 1p 1dc, 3dc in next sp, 3ch, skip 2sps; repeat from * right round work, ending with 2dc, close with sl st.

2nd rnd: 5ch, 3dbl tr cl in picot, * 5ch, 1dc in centre of 5dc, 5ch, 3dbl tr cl in picot, 1dbl tr in next sp, 3dbl tr cl in picot; repeat from * to corner, 5ch, 1dc in centre of 5dc, 5ch, 3dbl tr cl in picot, 5ch, 1dc in centre of 5dc, 5ch, 3dbl tr cl in picot, 5ch; work second side of heading to correspond with first side, close with sl st.

3rd rnd: 7dc in 5ch 1p, 1dc in cluster, 4ch, 1tr in next st, *5ch, 1tr in dc, 5ch, 1tr in cl, 1ch, 1tr in cl; repeat from * to corner, 7dc in 5ch 1p, 1dc in dc, 7dc in 5ch lp, 4ch, 1tr in cl; work other side to correspond, close with sl st.
Fasten off.

Trellis Edging

This edging matches the lace insertion pattern above. This beautiful set of insertion and matching edge is ideal for bed linen or any household item requiring lace.

Edging

Work edging the same as insertion until one side of heading is completed.

Scalloped Edge

* (3ch 2dc in next sp) 4 times, 2dc, 2dc in same sp, (3ch 2dc) 3 times; repeat from * to end of row, close with sl st.
Fasten off.

Mosaic

Commence with 31ch (29 + 3).

1st row: 1tr in 8th ch from hook, 2ch, skip 2ch, 1tr in next ch, 2ch, skip 2ch, 4tr, 2ch, skip ch, 4tr, (2ch, skip 2ch, 1tr in next ch) 3 times, 5ch, turn.

2nd row: 1tr in 2nd tr, 2ch, 1tr in next tr, 1tr in each of next 2ch, 4tr, 2ch, 4tr, 1tr in each of next 2ch, (1tr, 2ch) twice, 1tr in third of 5ch lp, 5ch, turn.

3rd row: 1tr in second tr, 2ch, 1tr in next tr, (2ch, skip 2tr, 1tr in next tr) twice, 1tr in each of next 2ch, (1tr, 2ch) 4 times, 1tr, 5ch, turn.

4th row: 1tr in second tr, 2ch, 1tr in tr, (1tr in each of next 2ch, 1tr in tr) twice, 2ch, skip 2tr, 1tr in next tr, (1tr in each of next 2ch, 1tr in tr) twice, (2ch, 1tr) twice, 5ch, turn.

5th row: 1tr in second tr, 2ch, 1tr, 2ch, 4tr, 2ch, 4tr, (2ch, 1tr in next tr) 3 times, 5ch, turn.

6th row: as 3rd row.

7th row: as 5th row.

8th row: as 3rd row.

Repeat these 8 rows for length required.
Fasten off.

Leaf and Bar

This wide insertion is worked in fillet crochet (instructions for fillet crochet appear on page 44.

Commence with 64ch.

1st row: 1tr in 4th ch from hook, 1tr in next ch, * 2ch, skip 2ch, 1tr in next ch; repeat from * 7 times (8 spaces), 1tr in each of next 6ch, 2ch, skip 2ch, 1tr in each of next 7ch, 2sps, 1tr in each of last 3ch, 3ch, turn (3ch is for 1st tr of next row).

2nd row: 2tr, 3sps, 13tr, 4sps, 4tr, 7sps, 3tr, 3ch, turn.

3rd row: 2tr, 7sps, 7tr, 2sps, 4tr, 2sps, 7tr, 3sps, 3tr, 3ch, turn.

4th row: 2tr, 3sps, 4tr, 3sps, 7tr, 1sp, 7tr, 7sps, 3tr, 3ch, turn.

5th row: 2tr, 7sps, 7tr, 1sp, 7tr, 3sps, 4tr, 3sps, 3tr, 3ch, turn.

6th row: 2tr, 3sps, 4tr, 3sps, 7tr, 1sp, 7tr, 7sps, 3tr, 3ch, turn.

7th row: 2tr, 5sps, 4tr, 1sp, 7tr, 1sp, 7tr, 2sps, 4tr, 4sps, 3tr, 3ch, turn.

8th row: 2tr, 4sps, 4tr, 2sps, 7tr, 1sp, 7tr, 1sp, 4tr, 5sps, 3tr, 3ch, turn.

9th row: 2tr, 4sps, 4tr, 2sps, 7tr, 1sp, 7tr, 1sp, 4tr, 5sps, 3tr, 3ch, turn.

10th row: 2tr, 5sps, 4tr, 1sp, 7tr, 1sp, 7tr, 2sps, 4tr, 4sps, 3tr, 3ch, turn.

11th row: 2tr, 3sps, 4tr, 3sps, 7tr, 1sp, 7tr, 7sps, 3tr, 3ch, turn.

12th row: 2tr, 7sps, 7tr, 1sp, 7tr, 3sps, 4tr, 3sps, 3tr, 3ch, turn.

13th row: 2tr, 3sps, 4tr, 3sps, 7tr, 1sp, 7tr, 7sps, 3tr, 3ch, turn.

3rd rnd: 7dc in 5ch 1p, 1dc in cluster, 4ch, 1tr in next st, *5ch, 1tr in dc, 5ch, 1tr in cl, 1ch, 1tr in cl; repeat

14th row: 2tr, 7sps, 7tr, 1sp, 4tr, 3sps, 7tr, 3sps, 3tr, 3ch, turn.

15th row: 2tr, 4sps, 13tr, 3sps, 4tr, 7sps, 3tr, 3ch, turn.

16th row: 2tr, 8sps, 19tr, 5sps, 3tr, 3ch, turn.

17th row: 2tr, 4sps, 4tr, 1sp, 19tr, 7sps, 3tr, 3ch, turn.

18th row: 2tr, 9sps, 7tr, 1sp, 4tr, 1sp, 7tr, 3sps, 3tr, 3ch, turn.
19th row: 2tr, 3sps, 10tr, 1sp, 22tr, 5sps, 3tr, 3ch, turn.
20th row: 2tr, 4sps, 19tr, 2sps, 4tr, 1sp, 7tr, 3sps, 3tr, 3ch, turn.
21st row: 2tr, 4sps, 4tr, 1sp, 10tr, 2sps, 7tr, 6sps, 3tr, 3ch, turn.

22nd row: 2tr, 4sps, 10tr, 1sp, 4tr, 1sp, 16tr, 4sps, 3tr, 3ch, turn.
23rd row: 2tr, 5sps, 4tr, 1sp, 16tr, 1sp, 10tr, 3sps, 3tr, 3ch, turn.
24th row: 2tr, 4sps, 4tr, 1sp, 19tr, 7sps, 3tr, 3ch, turn.
Repeat from first row for length required.
End with a 12th row.

Lace Edgings

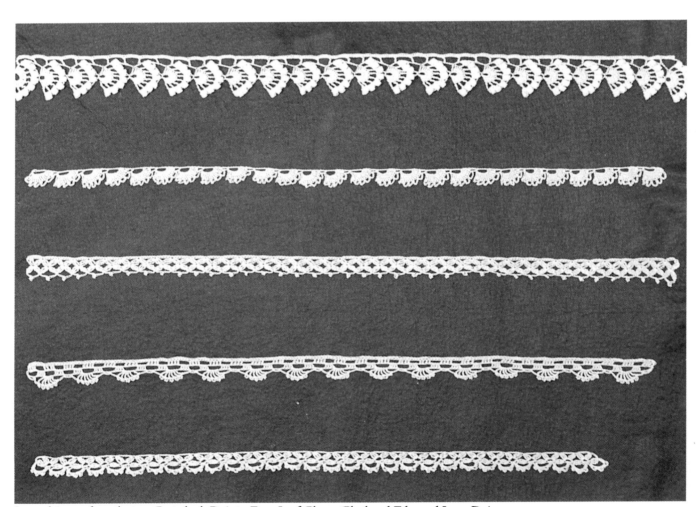

Lace edgings—from the top, Cartwheel, Dainty, Four-Leaf Clover, Checkered Edge and Lazy Daisy

Cartwheel

Commence with 10ch, close with sl st to form a ring.
1st row: 3ch, 14tr in ring, 5ch, turn.
2nd row: skip 1tr, 1tr in next tr, ★ 2ch, skip 1tr, 1tr in next tr; repeat from ★ 4 more times, 2ch, skip 1tr, 1tr in third of turning ch, 3ch, turn.
3rd row: ★ 7tr in next sp, drop lp from hook, insert hook in 3rd lp of chain and draw dropped lp through (popcorn st made), 3ch; repeat from ★ ending with a popcorn st in last sp, 10ch, turn.
4th row: skip 2sps, 1dc in next sp, 5ch, 1dc in same sp, 3ch, turn.
5th row: 13tr in 5ch lp, 1dc in 10ch lp, 5ch, turn.
Repeat 2nd to 5th rows till length required. Do not break yarn but work across one long side as follows:
1st row: ★ 1tr in next 10ch lp, 5ch, skip next popcorn, 1tr in next sp, 5ch; repeat from ★ to end of row, 1ch, turn.
2nd row: 7dc over each lp, 1dc in tr.
Fasten off.

Dainty Trim

Commence with 11ch.
1st row: 1tr in 11th ch from hook, 3ch, turn.
2nd row: 11tr in sp, 1tr in 4th ch made, 1ch, turn.
3rd row: 1dc in each tr, 1dc in top of turning ch (13dc in all), 5ch, turn.
4th row: skip first 2dc, 1dc in next dc, ★ 5ch, skip 1dc, 1dc in next dc; repeat from ★ 3 more times, 2ch, skip next dc, 1tr in next dc, 10ch, turn.
5th row: 1dc in next lp, 3ch, turn.
6th row: 11tr in sp, 1tr in 4th of 10ch counting from the tr below, 1ch, turn.
Repeat 3rd to 6th rows for length required.

Four-Leaf Clover

Work a chain for length required.
1st row: 1dc in each chain.
2nd row: 2tr tr in first dc leaving the last st of each tr on hook, ★ skip 5dc, 2tr tr in next dc having now 5lps on the hook, draw all 5lps through at once, 5ch, in same sp as last 2tr tr work 1sl st, 5ch, 2tr tr in same place leaving 3lps on hook; repeat from ★ ending with 5dc, in next work 3tr tr leaving 6lps on hook, draw all 6lps through at once, 5ch, turn.

3rd row: into st of cluster work 2tr tr tog, ★ 7ch, 1dc in third ch (picot made), 2ch, in same place work 3tr tr leaving 4lps on hook, into cluster work 3tr tr now having 7lps on hook, draw all 7lps through at once; repeat from ★ ending with 7ch, 1dc in 3rd ch, 2ch, 3tr tr tog.
Fasten off.

Checkered Edge

Work a chain for the length required.
1st row: 1dc into each ch, 3ch, turn.
2nd row: 1tr in each of next 3dc, ★ 3ch, skip 3dc, 1tr in each of next 4dc; repeat from ★, 4ch, turn.
3rd row: 4tr in 3ch sp, ★ 4ch, 4tr in next 3ch sp; repeat from ★, ending with 3ch, 1tr in last tr of previous row, turn.
4th row: in sp work 1dc 3ch 1dc, ★ 3ch, in each sp work 1dbl tr, 4ch, 1dc in 4th ch (picot made), 5 times, 1dbl tr, 3ch, in next sp work 1dc 3ch 1dc; repeat from ★ to end of row.
Fasten off.

Lazy Daisy

Commence with 10ch.
1st row: 3dbl tr cl in 10th ch from hook, 5ch, turn.
2nd row: 1tr in top of cl, 10ch, turn.
3rd row: work a dbl tr cl in top of last tr, 5ch, turn.
Repeat 2nd and 3rd rows for length required, ending with a 3dbl tr cl, 5ch.
Work along one long edge as follows:
★ into next 5ch lp work 3dbl tr cl 5ch 3dbl tr cl; repeat from ★ to end of row, 5ch, 1sl st in base of first cl made.
Now work along opposite edge as follows:
Into next 10ch lp work (3dc, 3ch) 3 times, 3dc, 1dc between lps; repeat from ★ to end of row.
Fasten off.

Braids

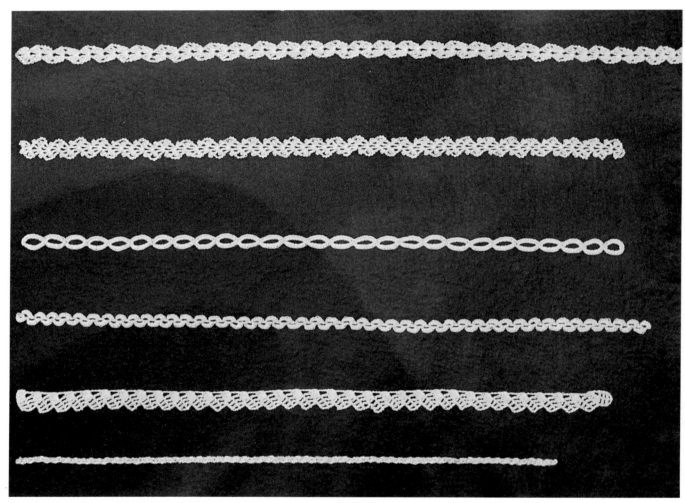

Braids—from the top, Shell, Lace, Ring, Crescent, Pointed Edge and Caterpillar

Shell

Simple shells worked in a narrow strip make this attractive braid. Make it either in a very thin cotton to decorate a blouse, or in thick cotton or wool to decorate home furnishing items.

Commence with 4ch, close with sl st to form a ring.
1st row: 3ch, 3tr in circle, 2ch, 4tr in same circle.
2nd row: 3ch, 3tr in 2ch lp, 2ch, 3tr in same 2ch lp, 1tr in turning ch, 3ch, turn.
These two rows form the pattern; repeat them for the length required.

Lace

Commence with 6ch.
1st row: 1tr in 6th ch from hook, 3ch, 1sl st in top of last tr (picot made), 1tr, 2ch, 1tr in same ch as last tr, 1p, 1tr in same ch of last tr, 5ch, turn.
2nd row: 1tr in 2ch sp of previous row, 1p, 1tr 2ch 1tr in same 2ch sp, 1p, 1tr in same 2ch sp, 5ch, turn.
Repeat 2nd row for length required.

Ring

This attractive braid is made by working dc in a ring on one side only, then turning your work and working back in the same way to complete the ring. If you alter the amount of chain and double crochet, you can make the rings larger or smaller.

Commence with 12ch, close with sl st to form a ring.
1st rnd: 8dc over one side of the ring, working from right to left, taking care not to twist the chain circle.
2nd rnd: make another 12ch, sl st into first ch, so making another circle, 8dc in this ring as for the first one. In this way make rings for the length required, working one side of the rings only.
Turn the braid so that the unworked side of the rings is at the top. Work 8dc along this side of the braid, and 1dc between the rings. Close with sl st in first dc to complete the first ring.
Fasten off.

Crescent

This pretty braid is worked over a small number of chain stitches, turning the work each time to achieve the double sided scallop effect. A narrow ribbon threaded through the holes looks very effective.

Commence with 5ch, close with sl st to form a ring.
1st rnd: 6dc over ring.
2nd rnd: 4ch, 1dc in last ring, turn your work so that the 4ch lp just made is at the beginning of the round.
3rd rnd: 6dc in this 4ch lp.
Turn and repeat rows 2 and 3 for length required, ending with 6dc in the last 4ch lp, close with sl st.

Pointed Edge

Commence with 10ch.
1st row: 1tr in 6th ch from hook, 1ch, skip 1ch, 1tr in next ch, 1ch, skip 1ch, in last ch work 1tr 1ch 1tr, 4ch, turn.
2nd row: skip first tr, (1tr in next tr, 1ch) twice, 1tr in next tr, 5tr in last sp, 5ch, turn.
3rd row: 1tr in first tr, (1ch, skip 1tr, 1tr in next tr) twice, 1tr in next sp, 4ch, turn.
Repeat 2nd and 3rd rows for length required.

Caterpillar

This very narrow braid has many uses. You may want to use it as a cord, or made in a thicker yarn to trim clothes or household items.

Commence with 2ch.
Work 1dc in first ch, twist the work half a turn to the left (clockwise, that is away from your body), and work a dc st in the second of the first 2ch (the lp at the top of the work).
Turn the work again in clockwise direction and work a dc st in the first of the 2 lps which come over the braid.
Continue to turn the braid each time after working the dc st, until you have the required length.
Complete the braid by drawing the yarn through all 3 lps at once when working the last dc.
You can make the braid thicker by working the hook through both the top lps, instead of one.

Bibliography

Australian Book of Crochet, published by Paul Hamlyn, Australia, 1972.

Crochet to Treasure, Family Circle Publication, 1992.

Needlecraft Practical Journal, published by Needlecraft Ltd, Manchester and London.

The Craft of the Crochet Hook, edited by Flora Klickman, the Office of Girl's Own Paper and Woman's Magazine, London.

The Fillet Crochet Book, by Chris Rankin, Sterling Publishing Co Inc, New York, 1990.

The Home Art Crochet Book, edited by Flora Klickman, the Office of "The Girl's Own Paper and Woman's Magazine, London.

Weldon's Practical Needlework, published by the Proprietors, Weldon's Ltd, Fashion, Pattern and Transfer Publisher, London.

Index